Ireland 1828–1923
From Ascendancy to Democracy

D. George Boyce

BLACKWELL
Oxford UK & Cambridge USA

Copyright © D. George Boyce 1992

The right of D. George Boyce to be identified as author of this work has been
asserted in accordance with the Copyright, Designs and Patents Act 1988.

First published 1992

Blackwell Publishers
108 Cowley Road
Oxford OX4 1JF
UK

238 Main Street, Suite 501
Cambridge, Massachusetts 02142
USA

British Library Cataloguing in Publication Data
A CIP catalogue record for this book is available from the British Library.

Library of Congress Cataloging-in-Publication Data

Boyce, David George, 1942–
    Ireland 1828–1923 : from ascendancy to democracy / D. George Boyce.
    123p.   cm.—(Historical Association studies)
    ISBN 0–631–18103–2 (alk. paper).—ISBN 0–631–17283–1 (pbk. : alk.
paper)
    1. Ireland—History—19th century. 2. Ireland—History—20th century. I.
Title. II. Series.
DA950.B677   1992
941.5081—dc20   92–11474
                                                                      CIP

Phototypeset in 11 on 13 pt Ehrhardt by Intype Limited

Printed in Great Britain by TJ Press Ltd, Padstow, Cornwall

This book is printed on acid-free paper

Historical Association Studies

Ireland 1828–1923

Historical Association Studies

General Editors: Muriel Chamberlain and H. T. Dickinson

China in the Twentieth Century
Paul Bailey

The Agricultural Revolution
John Beckett

Class, Party and the Political System in
Britain 1867–1914
John Belchem

The Ancien Régime
Peter Campbell

Decolonization: The Fall of the
European Empires
M. E. Chamberlain

Gandhi
Anthony Copley

The Counter-Reformation
N. S. Davidson

British Radicalism and the French
Revolution
H. T. Dickinson

From Luddism to the First Reform
Bill: Reform
in England 1810–1832
J. R. Dinwiddy

Radicalism in the English Revolution
1640–1660
F. D. Dow

British Politics Since 1945: The Rise
and Fall of Consensus
David Dutton

The Spanish Civil War
Sheelagh M. Ellwood

Revolution and Counter-Revolution in
France 1815–1852
William Fortescue

The New Monarchy: England,
1471–1534
Anthony Goodman

The French Reformation
Mark Greengrass

Britain and European Cooperation
Since 1945
Sean Greenwood

Politics in the Reign of Charles II
K. H. D. Haley

Occupied France: Collaboration and
Resistance 1940–1944
H. R. Kedward

Secrecy in Britain
Clive Ponting

Women in an Industrializing Society:
England 1750–1880
Jane Rendall

Appeasement
Keith Robbins

Franklin D. Roosevelt
Michael Simpson

Britain's Decline: Problems and
Perspectives
Alan Sked

The Cold War 1945–1965
Joseph Smith

Britain in the 1930s
Andrew Thorpe

Bismarck *Bruce Waller*

The Russian Revolution 1917–1921
Beryl Williams

Lloyd George
Chris Wrigley

The Historical Association, founded in 1906, brings together people who share an interest in, and love for, the past. It aims to further the study and teaching of history at all levels: teacher and student, amateur and professional. This is one of over 100 publications available at preferential rates to members. Membership also includes journals at generous discounts and gives access to courses, conferences, tours and regional and local activities. Full details are available from The Secretary, The Historical Association, 59a Kennington Park Road, London SE11 4JH, telephone: 071–735 3901.

For Maria and Niall

Contents

List of Abbreviations   viii

Acknowledgements   ix

1   Introduction: From Protestant Nation to Catholic
    Nation, 1690–1828   1

2   Reform and Romanticism, 1829–1846   15

3   The Famine, the Fenians and Gladstone, 1846–1870   30

4   The Politics of Home Rule, 1870–1893   45

5   Makers of a New Ireland, 1891–1910   62

6   Nationalism versus Unionism, 1911–1918   79

7   The Division of the Spoils, 1919–1923   94

8   Conclusion: Ascendancy and Democracy   109

References and Further Reading   112

Index   118

Abbreviations

ICA   Irish Citizen Army
IRA   Irish Republican Army
IRB   Irish Republican Brotherhood
IVF   Irish Volunteer Force
NHI   *New History of Ireland*
PRONI   Public Record Office of Northern Ireland
RIC   Royal Irish Constabulary
SPOI   State Paper Office of Ireland
UVF   Ulster Volunteer Force

Acknowledgements

I am grateful to the Marquis of Downshire for permission to quote from the Downshire Papers on page 6. I am also grateful to Dr A. P. W. Malcolmson for his unfailing assistance in tracing copyright owners.

1

Introduction: From Protestant Nation to Catholic Nation, 1690–1828

Nineteenth-century Ireland can only be understood in terms of the century that preceded it. Between 1690 and 1828 Irish history is largely the history of the Protestant minority of Ireland. Until the last decades of the eighteenth century the Irish Protestants, Anglican (Church of Ireland) and Dissenter (mostly Presbyterian), were the political nation, yet comprised about a quarter of the total population. At the top of the pyramid, and dominating the political and social scene were the Anglican (Church of Ireland) landlords, some 5,000 in number. They were in many respects a typical oligarchy of the Augustan age. Their power was based on their almost complete monopoly of landed property; their Church was the state Church, by law established; their country houses expressed power as well as style and taste; their children undertook the Grand Tour; and the political and administrative institutions of the country were in their hands, and theirs alone.

They had won their power in a kind of joint enterprise with the Whig oligarchy that ruled England after the climactic events of the Glorious Revolution of 1688–9, which established a Protestant king and constitution; for the corollary of that victory was the foundation of a Protestant kingdom and constitution in Ireland. Only thus could Ireland be made secure, and the British Isles made safe. The overthrow of James II after his defeat at the battle of the Boyne in July 1690 was quickly followed by a Protestant triumph over the whole of Ireland. Once safe, King William III's instinct was to ensure as fair a treatment for his Roman Catholic Irish subjects as was compatible with the well-being of the sister kingdoms. But he underestimated the fears of the Irish Protestants and their determination to assert their own interests. The post-revolutionary Irish Parliament showed a disposition to take the initiative when it came to framing the penal legislation that would keep the Roman Catholic enemy in his place – for good. William had no desire to pry into private conscience or make men choose between political and spiritual loyalty (Mitchison, 1982, p. 279); but his essentially eighteenth-century concept of his subjects contrasted with the seventeenth-century views of the Irish Protestants, who had learnt their lessons about loyalty and religion in a hard school.

William was faced with the same problem in Ireland as in Scotland: a Parliament dominated by a political/religious group (Anglican in Ireland, Presbyterian in Scotland) that insisted upon having matters its own way when it came to dealing with its recalcitrant rivals. In Scotland the enemies were Catholics and Episcopalians, in Ireland Catholics and Dissenters. The Irish Parliament was determined to ensure that it would never again suffer the Protestant interest being endangered. Its vigorous assertion of its rights appears odd in the light of its intermittent history; only four Parliaments met in Ireland between 1603 and 1688. But the Irish Protestants lived in special circumstances. First, they were a minority in the country, with little time for the luxury of toleration. Then they could, and did, fall back upon the idea that Ireland was an ancient kingdom with prescriptive rights. The Irish Parliament quickly developed a sense of its own importance for, after all, the English interest in Ireland depended upon the Protestant character of that Parliament.

This Parliament gave a continuity to the political life of eighteenth-century Ireland. It provided the forum for the opinions of the Protestants of Ireland; later on it became the focus of Protestant patriotic feeling; finally it was at the centre of the question of political reform until its abolition in 1800. But when

2

it met in 1692 its purpose was to make secure the victory won by force of arms in 1690. This desire for security produced one of the most paradoxical aspects of Protestant political thinking: the willingness to link liberty to the necessity of keeping Catholic power in permanent check and subjugation.

The plain truth, as Protestants saw it, was that compromise was impossible, at least in the public sphere; privately, many Protestants could, and did, make all kinds of accommodations with their Catholic neighbours. But the public sphere had profound implications for the lives of Roman Catholics, or at least for those who might have exercised political power through their rank and status. Between 1692 and 1704 Roman Catholics were deprived of the right to inherit land. They were excluded from public life and from the professions. They lost the right to carry arms (though Catholic gentlemen bore swords for some fifty years after these laws). They could not own horses above a certain value. Catholic bishops and regular clergy were banished, and Catholics were barred from foreign seats of learning. In 1728 all Catholics lost the right to vote. Protestant Dissenters too were penalized through sacramental tests and oaths of allegiance and abjuration.

But Protestants were less interested in driving out popery than in political security, and land was the basis of power. Despite the Williamite wars, Roman Catholics still possessed land. By 1703 their share had fallen to 14 per cent; eventually it fell to 5 per cent. But a Catholic gentry still existed, and later it would provide significant political leadership.

The penal laws had the effect of downgrading the Catholic Irish and, though to a much lesser degree, the Protestant Dissenters. Membership of the Church of Ireland was a necessary entry card for admission to any role in public life and polite society. The Church of Ireland was not a proselytizing or 'Enthusiastic' Church. It was, rather, the basis of a culture: Protestantism, progressiveness, Britishness, liberty of conscience and a superior outlook were its hallmarks. Its best advocate was Jonathan Swift, who put the case for a state Church as a defence of the kingdom against not only Catholics

3

but also Dissenters, that 'Babel of Sectaries' (Davis, 1955, pp. 285–95).

The security of Irish Protestants depended on their monopoly of landed power, on a state Church and on a Protestant Parliament for a Protestant nation. It also depended upon the English connection. But the Irish Parliament was conscious of its rights, and Swift again put the case for the Parliament and nation: Ireland was an ancient kingdom, and no mere Virginia, no petty colonial appendage.

The idea of the rights of Ireland was of only minor significance for most of the eighteenth century, and at times was cynically exploited as a political parrot-cry. But it was given force by the political dispute between England and her American colonies in the 1760s and 1770s, which aroused public interest in Ireland. American Radical Protestant ideas, which linked liberty with Dissent, were bound to strike up an interest among Presbyterians in Ireland, but even the Irish political establishment was affected by the crisis, for it gave the 'patriot' group in the Irish Parliament and in the country an opportunity to assert what they regarded as the rights of Ireland against the vexatious domination of the Parliament of England. This political excitement was given a new, and potentially dangerous, form in the Volunteer movement, founded in 1778 to protect Irish shores against possible invasion from the enemies of Britain, but with a powerful radical political element in its ranks. The Irish 'patriots' had the advantage of allies in the British parliament, and it was this, as much as the semi-military leverage of the Irish Volunteers, that created the 'revolution of 1782', when the Irish Parliament gained the right to initiate its own legislation, and the repeal of the Declaratory Act of 1719 by which the English Parliament had asserted its right to legislate over the head of the Irish Parliament.

The 'Constitution of 1782' reflected the views of the more progressive members of the Irish Protestant nation, and especially those of Henry Grattan. He was typical of that strand of Protestant thinking that held that the British connection, however modified, was essential for Ireland's prosperity: that while the sea forbade union, the ocean forbade separation;

hence his assumption that Ireland must be a sister kingdom, not a separate nation, and his acceptance of the English Privy Council's veto on Irish legislation. He also assumed that, however enlightened Irish Protestants might be in their attitude towards Roman Catholics, they would, and must, continue to dominate Ireland politically. These assumptions about the British connection and the Protestant interest were to be challenged in the last two decades of the eighteenth century.

For most of the eighteenth century the Roman Catholics and Dissenters of Ireland found themselves excluded from any significant part of the political process. Now they too began to involve themselves in the questions of the day, especially those concerning citizens' rights and the reform of the constitution. Presbyterians could see a common cause with the American radicals, especially since Dissenters had emigrated to America in large numbers in search of civil and religious freedom. In the Volunteer movement northern Presbyterians were prominent, and Volunteer companies were a kind of political club, whose members liked to debate the great issues of the day. Some Volunteer companies, especially those in Kerry, Cork and Armagh, admitted Roman Catholics. There was another incentive to test the strength of the Protestant establishment, for now the British government, anxious to reconcile disaffected citizens, began to steer relief measures through the Irish parliament, using all its resources of influence and control over Irish MPs. In 1778 a Relief Act removed restrictions on Catholics holding land; in 1782 Gardiner's Relief Act liberalized the position of education, marriage and property, while forbidding Catholics to buy land in parliamentary boroughs where their political influence might be asserted.

This new political climate offered a serious test to the Irish Parliament in an age when Parliament was the focus of political life. It also saw a similar debate in the British Parliament, based on the same question: could the constitution bequeathed by the Glorious Revolution be reformed to remedy its perceived deficiencies? Or were more radical measures of reform called for? In Ireland, the debate was complicated by the fragmented nature of Irish society. An Englishman was an Englishman,

5

even if, as a Dissenter, his views were mistrusted on many political issues. But the Irish Catholic was feared and mistrusted, for his religion and politics were deemed incompatible with the very root and branch of the constitution. And an Irish Dissenter was not merely a member of a troublesome minority. In Ulster, he was part of a fixed and numerically strong local people, whose hopes of political power, frustrated in 1690, might now be reasserted. But at least the Protestants could take comfort in the reflection that, if Dissenters resented their privileges, then they feared any restoration of Roman Catholic power even more.

But in the 1790s it seemed that Dissenters – or a sizeable number of them – no longer feared to challenge the political monopoly of the ascendancy. Tom Paine's radical writings proved such best sellers in Ireland that one staunch defender of the constitution complained to the Marquis of Downshire

> Is it not a shame to government, to their Graces and my Lords, the Archbishops and Bishops of this land, that it was left to the munificence, public spirit and religious principle of a private citizen of Belfast to print and publish at his own expense 1,500 sixpenny copies of Bishop Watson's 'Apology for the Bible' in order to contend with the cheap editions of Payne's [sic] 'Age of Reason' that are industriously circulated throughout the country. (PRONI, Downshire Papers, D 607/D/180, James Arbuckle to Downshire, 18 September 1796)

But Church of Ireland men were by no means all hostile to the new ideas. Some of them, notably Theobald Wolfe Tone, a young Protestant with an eye to radical politics, were prepared to throw their lot in with the radical cause. Tone, who spent a short time in America, did not find that country to his liking, but, like a good radical, he put all the blame on government. If you meet a 'confirmed blackguard', he wrote, 'you may be sure he is Irish'; but, he added, the blame for this must be put on the 'execrable government at home', for when the Irish went to America and found themselves well treated then 'their heads

6

are turned' (Hobson, n.d., p. 46–7).

Yet the Irish, or at least the hitherto excluded portion of them, were now receiving close and favourable attention from the British government, anxious to enlist their sympathy in the war with revolutionary France. In 1793 Roman Catholics were admitted to the franchise on the same terms as Protestants (but still debarred from positions of political power). This decision was criticized, in retrospect, by the Protestant historian and political writer W. E. H. Lecky, on the grounds that it gave political power to Catholic masses while withholding from their proper representatives the means of influencing it. With no Catholic gentry leadership, the masses were vulnerable to radical demagogues (Lecky, 1912, pp. 150–5). Certainly Roman Catholic expectations had been raised; and the next step – the right to sit in Parliament – had some sympathy in British official circles. But there were those, like Lord Castlereagh, who held that the admission of Roman Catholics to full political rights was not compatible with Protestantism, and therefore the safety of the British Isles. 'Can,' he asked, 'the Protestant Church remain the Establishment of a State of which they do not comprise an eighth part, which will be the case when the Catholics are co-equal in political rights?' Dissenters, he conceded, were a problem; but not as serious a problem as Roman Catholics. And the difference was this: enemies within and without the state 'tell very differently. The one destroys by *legislation*, the other by *rebellion*' (Derry, 1976, pp. 37–8). Castlereagh's speculation comprises the history of Ireland in the nineteenth century, except that the destruction of the establishment was by legislation, not rebellion, as the British state sought to reconstruct Irish society to bind Ireland to the Union with England.

But for the moment rebellion seemed to be the preferred option of both Catholics and Dissenters, or at least some of them. Roman Catholic hopes of emancipation were raised in 1795, when a new viceroy, Lord Fitzwilliam, came to Ireland with an earnest, if somewhat over-optimistic, desire to change Dublin Castle and Ireland for the better. Fitzwilliam overstepped the mark, and the government felt obliged to recall him. But this only thrust many Roman Catholics into a society founded in

1791 in Belfast and Dublin to push on the pace of reform: the United Irishmen. Wolfe Tone, whose opinion of government was expressed in frank terms, and other leading members of the United Irishmen resolved on more desperate means to bring Ireland the benefits of the Enlightenment. Tone now blamed not only government for Ireland's ills, but the whole English connection. The logical conclusion – an independent Irish republic – was a breathtaking step, one never contemplated before but one liable to meet with stern resistance, frightening the less bold spirits among both Catholics and Dissenters as well. Even committed radicals were anxious lest Roman Catholics, 'dreamers about ancient possessions', would seek to pursue the forbidden path of reversing the verdict of 1690, thus seeing a restoration of their property and power (Jones, 1792, p. 16).

This growing fragmentation of the radical front explains the almost incoherent nature of the 1798 rebellion in Ireland, which was really a series of discrete and separate risings in Wexford, Antrim, and finally the west. The Wexford outbreak, in May 1798, was a kind of Protestant–Catholic war on a small but murderous scale, as the Protestant Yeomanry and the Catholic rebels met atrocity with atrocity. In Antrim, Presbyterians rose with radical slogans on their lips and a whole host of grievances in their hearts, not least the repressive measures adopted by the British army and its ill-disciplined fencible regiments. In September the embers of revolt were stirred into life by the coming of the French, but in numbers too small to tip the scales against the Crown forces, who, aided by the Protestant Yeomanry and the Catholic Militia, took revenge for their humiliating defeat at Castlebar. The events of May to September 1798 only emphasized and deepened the differences between Catholics, Protestants and Dissenters; and even the differences within these groups, as the Catholic Church, the Presbyterian elders, and the vast bulk of Protestants condemned those of their number who became involved in the bloody risings and their consequences.

In 1800 a peace was imposed on Ireland by a British government anxious to secure its western flank in wartime. That peace was followed by an Act of Union between Great Britain and Ireland, secured by the younger Pitt after two years of intensive political pressure exerted on the Irish parliament. Most Roman Catholics supported the idea of Union, or were at least neutral towards it, for, after all, the British government had advanced their cause steadily before the débâcle of the Fitzwilliam episode in 1795. There was considerable Protestant opposition to Union. An Irish Parliament dominated by Protestants was, up to a point, master of its own fate, and there was also genuine Protestant patriotic sentiment about the 'Constitution of 1782'. But the anti-Unionists found themselves confronted by Pitt's secure majority in Westminster, and the knowledge that permanent opposition would mean the end of any possible future political career. Protestant resentment of the Union did not disappear overnight, but the most striking aspect of Protestant attitudes is the ready acceptance of Union, not merely as a political reality, but as a final and irrevocable settlement of Anglo-Irish affairs, and as a guarantee of their political survival in Ireland.

The main features of the Union, which came into effect on 1 January 1801, were that the Irish Parliament was dissolved, with Ireland now sending one hundred MPs to Westminster, and twenty-eight peers and four bishops to the House of Lords. These MPs, peers and bishops were grafted on to what was in origin the English Parliament, with its long history and traditions, and this would deeply influence the character of Irish politics as they developed in the nineteenth century. The Churches of England and Ireland were united, and this was regarded as an essential part of the making of the extended United Kingdom. The Protestant establishment, which was not only a religious one, but also a political and social group, was thus formally incorporated into the Union. Therefore, to attack that establishment in any of its forms was to attack the very basis of the Union, or so Protestants maintained. This placed Roman Catholics at a disadvantage. Not only must they convince British public opinion of the justice of their claims for full civil rights, but they must also persuade British opinion that

9

Catholic rights were compatible with the continuation of the United Kingdom.

This dilemma soon became apparent. Roman Catholics had hoped that the Union would be accompanied by Catholic emancipation (the right of Roman Catholics to sit in Parliament). But Pitt, though strongly in favour of emancipation, felt that he could not insist upon it against the wishes of King George III, who felt that emancipation was incompatible with his coronation oath to maintain the Protestant character of the constitution. This did not mean that the issue would die, for the tide of Roman Catholic feeling in the last decades of the eighteenth century was breaking down the passivity and deference which was a significant part of the basis of Protestant ascendancy. Within a few years the 'Catholic question', as it was called, resurfaced, but now it was placed firmly in the centre of Westminster politics.

Between 1808 and 1828 the question of emancipation absorbed much of Westminster's time and energy; and it is to be wondered at that such a securely Protestant institution as the British Parliament should have laboured so long on the issue. But it was precisely because England was such an overwhelmingly Protestant country that she found it hard to accept Roman Catholics in her Parliament: Roman Catholics who, for centuries, had been regarded as disloyal and even treasonable people. But the long-drawn-out nature of the controversy had important repercussions on Irish and British politics. In Ireland, the persistent frustration of Catholic hopes only prepared the way for a new, more forceful, agitation, led by the Catholic landowner and lawyer Daniel O'Connell, which threatened to remove the controversy from Westminster and make it the centre of Catholic popular opinion. This, in turn, overshadowed the persistent and sincere efforts of some liberal Protestants in the House of Commons to persuade the British Parliament to concede emancipation. Thus the liberal Protestant contribution to the cause was swept aside and the more aggressive (yet constitutional) style of O'Connell frightened Irish Protestants, who saw their worst nightmare about to come true – the replacement of a Protestant ascendancy by a Roman Catholic one.

10

Yet both Irish Catholics and Protestants had one experience in common: they were no longer the masters of their political destiny. They could pressurize, oppose, argue, even vote (in limited numbers); but they were all obliged to bring their grievances to Westminster, and persuade the political majority – the British political majority – to attend to their demands. They had, ultimately, little power, though at times a significant degree of political leverage, depending on the composition of the House of Commons. This easily produced a sense of frustration, unease, even betrayal among all Irish political groups at various times. Now the Catholic could feel let down; now the Protestant could feel compromised; now the Catholic could savour triumph; now the Protestant could enjoy the delights of victory. Yet all had good reason to feel discontented with their lot at some time or other, and one group's triumph was often necessarily regarded as the cause of the other's despair.

The liberal Protestant emancipationists believed that the Irish Catholic, once admitted to Parliament, would find himself surrounded by British and Protestant MPs and a British and Protestant environment that would give him means of redress, yet neutralize his power of making mischief. This dual policy was expressed in the 'veto', which had been raised as long ago as 1782. The veto was a safeguard for the British and Protestant tradition, in that it gave the British government the right to approve all episcopal appointments and thus ensure a hierarchy loyal to the Crown and state. Roman Catholics were divided on this issue, and in 1808, 1809 and 1810 they had discussed the veto, only to founder on the opposition of the more radical emancipationists, led by Daniel O'Connell, who held that to concede this right to a British government would drive a wedge between church and people in Ireland (*NHI*, V. i, 1989, pp. 36–44). In May 1813 the Catholic Board, established in 1811 to press the case for emancipation, considered Henry Grattan's emancipation bill, which included the veto, and again the arguments were plain: to accept it would be to place the Catholic hierarchy in the pocket of the British state, and deprive O'Connell and his followers of an important source of their political influence. To O'Connell, religion, nationality, and popular feeling were as one or must be as one, if the Catholics were ever to make good what he claimed was theirs by right of their status as the majority in the Irish nation. Liberal Protestants were of course welcome to join that nation, but they must not think of themselves as constituting the nation, as they had done in the last century. Thus, in his eyes, Protestants were, or would be, a permanent, if acceptable, minority.

O'Connell's achievement was to build on the kind of growing tide that had developed in the age of radicalism before 1800. His popular appeal was reinforced from several different angles. The early nineteenth century saw a period of economic distress in Ireland, a near famine in 1816–17, and a revival of agrarian secret societies whose activities posed a serious public-order problem. Then there was the vexed question of tithes for the upkeep of the Church of Ireland, which the Catholic population was required by law to pay and which it resented bitterly. O'Connell had no desire to encourage law-breaking. On the contrary, the whole idea of social or political disorder frightened him; he had no wish to speak of 1798. But he could incorporate a whole range of Catholic or rural grievances into his movement, control them, and aim them at the head of the British government. This gave him powerful political influence, even if the challenge was a dangerous one. He also played upon the sectarian passions that were surfacing in the new century, as Roman Catholics began to counter-attack the long-established Protestant supremacy. O'Connell had a broad and fairly tolerant eighteenth-century attitude to religion, but he had a nineteenth-century attitude to Protestantism, and he showed scant regard for the deep-seated fears of Protestants that, at bottom, Catholic triumph meant Protestant overthrow. These fears were fuelled by popular prophecies that 'Harry's breed' would be extirpated, that the hour of reckoning had come for the Protestants of Ireland.

In January 1824 O'Connell took what may fairly be regarded as one of the most important decisions in modern Irish history. He reduced the membership fee for the Catholic Association (the reformulated Catholic Board) from one guinea a year to as little as a penny a month. This enabled poorer Catholics to

12

join and identify closely with what might otherwise have seemed a remote cause. This, added to better organization and a more energetic leadership, allowed the Catholic Association to found its emancipation claim, not only on grounds of abstract justice – principles located in English political theory – but also on mass support and mass pressure; and to claim that the Catholics of Ireland were not only in a majority, but were *the* majority, whose just demands could not be denied. This mass following caught the attention and support of continental Europe, and made O'Connell one of the greatest figures of his age. Catholic claims were founded, not on English liberal theory, but on Irish demographic facts.

But this movement, however democratic in tone, was based upon the organization of the Roman Catholic Church, and especially the local clergy. O'Connell's instinct over the veto issue was vindicated, but, once more, liberal Protestants found themselves lying down with strange bedfellows, the more so as O'Connell was capable of denouncing Irish Protestants in one breath and praising the more liberal elements among them with the next. The fragility of O'Connell's relations with liberal Protestants was soon exposed. In 1825 he felt sure that victory was within his grasp, when he accepted a bill with 'wings' (i.e. special clauses), providing for the payment from public funds of salaries to Roman Catholic clergy, and also the abolition of the forty-shilling freeholder franchise (which included a large Roman Catholic vote). O'Connell had little faith in the independence of these freeholders and he accepted the 'wings', only to see this bill (Burdett's bill) rejected by the Lords by 178 votes to 130 (Boyce, 1990, p. 44).

O'Connell was now deeply compromised. But some of his local supporters in County Waterford resolved to test the mettle of the Catholic voters. In 1826 a group of Waterford liberals challenged the ruling Beresford family seat. The election was inspired by liberals, but quickly showed signs of sectarian feeling. Roman Catholics wore green handkerchiefs, sashes, cockades and ribbons. 'The constant cry is "High for Stuart [i.e. the deposed royal family of 1688] and Down with Lord George Beresford. Down with the Protestants",' wrote Major Robert

13

Willcock, who was in charge of the extra force of police in Waterford (Reynolds, 1954, p. 96). The emancipationists won and O'Connell was influenced by the victory, which showed the benefits of a well-organized and popular campaign. Other elections in 1826 revealed a similar trend.

Catholic Ireland was aroused and a rare unanimity was forged, as the drive towards emancipation intensified. In May 1828 Daniel O'Connell was persuaded to stand for election in County Clare. This was not a direct defiance of the law, but it was a symbolic protest against the oath MPs must take on entering Parliament, which was couched in terms offensive to the Catholic religion. And it was a challenge too to the liberal Protestants who held the Clare seat, the Vesey Fitzgeralds. Once again the Catholic clergy turned out in force, and Protestants witnessed the spectacle of Catholic triumphalism when O'Connell wrested the seat from Vesey Fitzgerald, who, acknowledging that he was bound to lose the contest, withdrew after five days of polling. The Clare victory was the signal for Catholic demonstrations, some of them of a dangerously military nature, all over Ireland. Catholics were right to celebrate, for the Clare election marked their progress from the degradation of the penal era to the breakdown of deference in the late eighteenth century, and on to the popular triumph of 1828. Protestants were right to tremble and resolve to concede no more, as they watched not only Protestant but landlord power defied, and their religion and traditions vilified. 1828, not 1800, marked the end of eighteenth-century Ireland. It also revealed that concepts like 'liberty' and 'democracy' had a special meaning in Ireland, for the Protestant idea of liberty meant a denial of Roman Catholic democracy and the Roman Catholic idea of democracy was incompatible with the Protestant idea of liberty. The two great political ideologies of the modern age were thus given a particular, and somewhat ominous, Irish dimension.

2

Reform and Romanticism, 1829–1846

O'Connell's victory in County Clare in June 1828 was not the only reason why the British government conceded Catholic emancipation. It was the culmination of a long and arduous campaign, and of the gradual weakening of the Protestant resolve to stand firm. There was also the fact that O'Connell's challenge was thrown down at the feet of a ministry which was at least half-committed to emancipation. When Parliament reassembled in February 1829 the King's speech contained the promise of Catholic relief; and by April a bill received the assent of both Houses of Parliament. Roman Catholics could now hold all offices of state, except those of regent, lord lieutenant and lord chancellor. Roman Catholic MPs need not take the oath of supremacy, but they were still obliged to deny the Pope's civil authority in the United Kingdom. This maintained a measure of distinction between Catholic and non-Catholic subjects, especially as MPs also had to deny any intention of subverting the existing settlement of the established church. And the doubtful nature of the British attitude towards Roman Catholics was expressed again in a measure passed at the same time, disenfranchising the forty-shilling freeholders in Ireland and creating a ten-pound franchise instead: a counter-attack on those who, it was held, were most dangerous to the political stability of Ireland. The Catholic Association was suppressed. This hardly consoled Protestant Conservative opinion, which claimed that a deadly blow had been delivered to its heart, and that the emigration of so many of the 'lower order of Protestants' meant that 'for the last eight or nine years, indeed ever since the year 1825, and more especially since the year 1829, the number has been swelling to such an extent, that it is utterly impossible for our Protestant population to supply so exhausting a drain much longer' (*Dublin University Magazine*, no. XIX, July 1834, p. 1).

This raised a question of vital importance for the Union between Great Britain and Ireland. Was its purpose to reform Ireland in such a way as to reconcile the Catholic majority to the Union, and thus create a new interest which would bind Ireland to Great Britain? Or was the Union designed to protect and succour an older interest, the Protestant one, that had already, and for some time, claimed that it was the only safe and secure means of achieving the same purpose? Both alternatives called for the steady and knowledgeable attention of the British government, but it was not yet clear that the Union would elicit this kind of response.

O'Connell, fresh from his victory in Clare, was uncertain of which way to go. His immediate call was for a new popular and clerical organization to work for the repeal of the Union and the restoration of the Irish Parliament, a measure regarded by Protestants as tantamount to their destruction and by the British government as a dismemberment of the empire. But he was a realist, and he was willing to concentrate on reform within the context of the Union. Reform raised one of the key problems of Ireland within the United Kingdom: the under-government of the country. The difficulty was that a *laissez-faire* aspiration broadly suited the growing economic and industrial prosperity of Great Britain, but Ireland lacked the basis for Britain's industrial growth and trading opportunities and she needed more, not less, state intervention. O'Connell was a Benthamite and had his doubts about the efficacy of state intervention as a principle of government action, but he was in favour of it if it would alleviate Irish rural distress and dismantle the Protestant ascendancy, with its monopoly of professional and public jobs.

Either way, the problem lay in gaining the attention of

Westminster. O'Connell's resources were limited, even though the 1830 general election gave him a parliamentary following of some thirty Repealers. He supported Lord Grey's Reform Bill of 1832; but he gained little from his exertions, for the Irish reform bill did not restore the forty-shilling freeholders' franchise, nor did Ireland gain as many new seats as O'Connell felt she was entitled to. The next few years revealed only frustration and disappointment. Parts of the Irish countryside were plunged into a state of terror as the tithe war raged, and Roman Catholics embarked on a vigorous and aggressive campaign against the payment of tithes to the Church of Ireland. In December 1831 twelve policemen were killed while serving tithe processes in County Kilkenny. Grey's government responded in 1832 with an act which made the commutation of tithes a fixed charge upon the land, with commissioners appointed by the incumbent to collect the amount that should be paid by the parish, a method first adopted in 1823. At the same time a sum of £60,000 was granted for the relief of the Protestant clergy rendered almost destitute by the failure to collect tithes. These expedients made the collection less abrasive, but the heart of the grievance was the system, not the method of collection. Leading Roman Catholic bishops condemned the system, while at the same time calling for an end to the tithe war. It made sense for the government to conciliate the bishops. In August 1832 the Irish Church Temporalities Act suppressed ten Church of Ireland bishoprics, reduced the revenues of the remaining twelve, and provided for the administration of the surplus revenue for ecclesiastical purposes.

Protestants were outraged at this high-handed treatment of their Church. At last they had suffered a taste of what a British government would do when it was placed in a difficult position, forced to set its face against the Protestant interest in order to conciliate the Catholic one. For their part, Catholics found the measure half-hearted and resented the application of the surplus money for church purposes. The welter of recrimination was repeated over another of Grey's reform measures, this time in educational policy. In 1831 the Whigs prepared the foundations for a national system of education in Ireland which would encompass children of all religious persuasions, while allowing for separate religious instruction. Catholics at first welcomed it; Anglicans and Presbyterians were hostile. Concessions to Protestant opinion aroused Catholic suspicion. In the event the overwhelming desire of each religious group to look after its own and protect its flock against the 'other sort' rendered the national schools essentially sectarian in character.

This was an unfortunate beginning to hopes of creating a consensus between Great Britain and Ireland, but within a short time O'Connell and the Whigs formed an alliance that seemed to promise a new and more positive experiment. O'Connell fought the 1835 general election on the question of repeal of the Union, but he quickly saw the advantages of making some kind of agreement with the Whigs, now led by Lord Melbourne. This would not only keep out the Conservatives but would also direct the Whigs into a more positive approach to Irish affairs. The first impact of the O'Connell–Whig alliance was felt in what had hitherto been the bastion of Protestant privilege, Dublin Castle. The man most closely associated with what might be called the 'Dublin Spring' of the 1830s was Thomas Drummond, under-secretary at the Castle; but he was ably supported by the chief secretary, Viscount Morpeth, in his efforts to demonstrate that the administration of Ireland did not exist merely for Protestant benefit. Judges, magistrates, police inspectors and legal officials were now drawn from the Catholic side. Irish landowners were reminded that property had its duties as well as its rights (an admonition, however, less frequently applied in the case of England). Above all, Drummond's tenure of office saw the Castle set its face against the Orange Order, a mainly rural Protestant organization founded in 1795 to protect Protestant interests and defend the constitution. The Order had in 1822 discredited itself by a rowdy demonstration in the Theatre Royal against the Lord Lieutenant, who had sought to dissuade it from decorating the statue of William III in Dublin. In 1825 it was obliged to dissolve itself, but it revived in 1828 and continued to flourish in Ireland, while never recovering its former position in Great Britain. Now the Order saw its demonstrations prohibited, sympathetic magistrates dis-

18

missed, and its very existence threatened. In April 1836 the Grand Orange Lodge ordered the organization to disband, and it did not revive until 1845.

The administration of Ireland had clearly adopted a new style, but devising laws to make Ireland a contented member of the United Kingdom proved more elusive. The reform of Irish municipal corporations was by any standards overdue: they were debt-ridden and possessed few real functions. But they were regarded as legitimate objects of Protestant control, and attempts to reform them met with stern Conservative opposition, which sought to limit the introduction of popular control. A commission of inquiry was set up in 1835, but reform was delayed until 1840, when fifty-eight corporations were dissolved, and the administration of the boroughs was merged with that of the counties. The remaining ten corporations were reconstituted, but with a more restricted ten-pound householder franchise; nor were the new corporations given control of the police.

Nevertheless, municipal reform produced at least one great symbolic result: the election of Daniel O'Connell as Lord Mayor of Dublin in November 1841. O'Connell was the first Roman Catholic to hold the office since the reign of James II, and it was symptomatic of the primacy of politics in Irish life that this should be the occasion of great celebrations on one side and profound misgivings on the other. Meanwhile, Ireland needed government, perhaps more than she needed politics, and the Whig government introduced important reforms in public health, sanitation and the management of the poor. The Irish Poor Law of 1838 revealed the advantages and disadvantages of British rule in Ireland. The government was at last addressing itself to the problem of the large number of the poor, and the consequent misery and degradation that resulted from their condition. It is doubtful if a native Irish government would have done more. But the disadvantage was seen in attempts to apply English remedies to an Irish defect, to set aside local advice and to act in a direct and high-handed manner.

The government's poor law was closely linked to its hostile

19

attitude to Irish landed property. Influential opinion tended to lay the blame for Ireland's economic ills, her poverty, her backwardness, at the door of the landlords, yet landlords would – O'Connell himself believed – be ruined by a poor rate which they could not afford. Ireland had more vagrants, and fewer solvent landlords, than England. Thus the 1833 Poor Law Commission, presided over by Richard Whately, Archbishop of Dublin, took account of Irish conditions and argued for a scheme which required a considerable injection of state capital. But, even as his Commission gathered information, Whately was becoming increasingly aware that the government had its own ideas of the kind of poor law it wanted. When these were not embodied in the Commission's report, the government produced its own scheme: one that set aside the notion of public works and state-sponsored employment and created instead an English-style workhouse system in Ireland, supported by a poor rate, half to be paid by the landlords in a poor law district, and half by the tenants (Boyce, 1990, pp. 69–71).

This poor law was aimed at forcing people out on to the market, where they would find employment, but Ireland had few opportunities to absorb this population. The system could not cope with poverty and destitution if Ireland was faced again – as she was in 1816 and 1817 – by a serious shortage of food; the scheme provided for an estimated workhouse population of some 80,000. While it is risky to judge retrospectively, in the light of the great famine of 1847–9, the system was defective in its whole conception of Irish poverty and society. But then Ireland had not been systematically conquered and reorganized, as many European countries had been. Few special institutions had been devised to meet her needs, and the piecemeal, English-inspired reforms of the Whigs were the best she could expect.

And yet there was a growing recognition that there existed something that might loosely be defined as an Irish question, and the existence and definition of that question owed much to the party with which O'Connell was most disposed to take issue: the Conservatives.

The Conservative leader, Sir Robert Peel, was unusual

among British politicians in that he had firsthand Irish experience (even if it earned him an 'Orange' reputation) as chief secretary for Ireland between 1812 and 1818. But, like all British political leaders, he had to cope with pressing domestic, foreign and imperial issues, and Ireland tended to fall into the gaps between these categories. If a problem was hard to define, then it was generally safer to leave it alone, for policy required clearing the ground, identifying the issues and formulating a coherent response. It was tempting, therefore, to leave Ireland to more ad hoc responses, especially as it seemed less amenable to any appreciable improvement. Yet Peel was aware of the value of what he called looking 'beyond the present', and he understood the importance of laying the foundations 'of a better state of things' (*NHI*, 1989, p. 182).

But the initiative was temporarily wrested from him by O'Connell's decision to resurrect the campaign for a repeal of the Union. O'Connell was caught in the dilemma that confronted leaders of the Catholic cause. To work his way into the British political system, through an alliance with a British political party, might provide material advantages, yet the British party would remain the senior partner in the agreement, and might not act in accordance with the best interests of the Irish party. To act as a demagogue, to rouse mass opinion, created an impression of power and charisma, but it raised the dangerous possibility of violence and disorder which O'Connell (like most Catholic leaders) sought fundamentally to limit and control. When he embarked on his repeal campaign in 1840, he could take comfort from the great, and controlled, pressure of 1828.

O'Connell had to create a sense of communal solidarity, even a sense of nationhood. This required organizational skill, but it also called for a millennial style, a great and popular appeal, a promise of a brave new world. O'Connell's magnificent oratory, in fluent Irish as well as impeccable English, provided the fuel and, after a slow start, the repeal campaign gathered momentum. He called upon the Catholic people to recall the great days of 1782, when 'the people of the land took courage' and rose up together, and Ireland was 'her own true self'. He urged his people not to 'suffer foreigners to rule' any longer. 'You will get your own parliament again and Ireland will be as she should be: the sap of her body nourishing herself.' A parliament in Dublin would give the people 'a million acres of land'. 'Give three cheers for O'Connell, the second Moses' (O Buachalla, 1970, pp. 84–94). The by now apparently unbreakable links between nationalism, democracy and Catholicism were expressed in the proceedings of a repeal meeting held in County Meath in December 1841. Toasts were offered to 'The People, the true source of all legitimate power'; 'The great bulwark of our liberties, the Press'; 'Their venerated and esteemed prelate, the Right Rev. Dr. Cantwell, and the Catholic Clergy' (*Weekly Freeman's Journal* 1 January 1842).

These links were now indeed well forged. Yet a group of young enthusiasts hoped to accompany O'Connell in his journey towards the promised land, and at the same time modify its character. They were led by a Protestant Irishman from County Cork, Thomas Davis, whose group was quickly dubbed (much to its annoyance) 'Young Ireland'. Young Ireland was Protestant in inspiration and in many ways conservative in disposition. It had no desire to alter the relations between the classes in Ireland; it had no wish to place a Catholic ascendancy in power. If Henry Grattan saw the nation as essentially Protestant, with Catholics added, and if O'Connell defined it as essentially Catholic, with Protestants added, then Davis wanted to transcend both these concepts and see it as a blend of the two. But part of his desire to create this new nation was based on his wish to secure a place for Protestants in Ireland.

Davis and his colleagues were faced with a formidable task. The heady days of Grattan were long past. Since 1820 Ireland had seen a sharpening, not only of political conflict, but the nourishing of its roots – the revival of deep sectarian divisions. Protestant, Presbyterian and Roman Catholic alike participated in the competition to secure the foundations of their respective religions and undermine those of their enemies. They discovered a new value in their church and an increasing fervour in their religious worship. 'Protestantism', as both a religion and a political concept, was given a solidarity that it had not known since the seventeenth century, and efforts were made to complete the task that the first reformation had left unfinished: the conversion of Catholic Ireland. Irish Protestant religion was always prone to lay great emphasis on the value of individual salvation, and was ever anxious about the power of Rome. It was not hard to make links between this and the political sentiment that feared Catholic power, hated Catholic solidarity and community feeling. Catholics responded with hostility, and some doubted whether a Protestant could be regarded as a member of the Christian Church. Again, this rejection of the other side had easy political parallels, as Catholic political solidarity rejected the idea that Protestants were in any real sense part of the 'Irish nation'. Parochial reorganization, the expansion of the numbers of the clergy and a new confidence created by the great emancipation campaign put the Catholic ranks into readiness for battle. There were always open-minded and liberal Protestants and Catholics; but the line between religion and politics was becoming harder to draw, and each side saw the other in menacing terms. Irish Catholics, more especially the priests but also the bishops, found it possible to distinguish between the sound doctrinal basis of Rome's concern over political involvement and the special conditions of Ireland. By 1843, after some initial hesitation, the hierarchy, led by Archbishop McHale of Tuam, put its shoulder to the repeal campaign.

But this time O'Connell and his supporters had miscalculated. No one in Great Britain would countenance the destruction of the Union. Unlike 1829, concession was not regarded as preferable to civil war. Peel spoke for England when he made it clear that he would stand his ground. When O'Connell threatened to defy him by holding a 'monster meeting' at Clontarf in October 1843 Peel prohibited the assembly and prepared to use force. O'Connell, who had already shown signs of wanting to turn from agitation to parliamentarianism, called off his meeting (*NHI*, 1989, p. 185). Peel now ordered O'Connell's arrest. The Liberator was subsequently imprisoned in Richmond jail, and although his incarceration was civil and mild, he never recovered his old fighting spirit.

Irish nationalism was now troubled by two developments.

23

One was its defeat by Peel in 1843; the other was Peel's determination to embark on a policy of reforms, which he hoped would genuinely help the Irish people, and especially the Catholics, but also draw the sting of nationalist sentiment. Irish nationalism had shifted its ground dramatically since 1782, and was now hardly recognizable as the nationalism of the Grattanite golden age. Roman Catholics were well on their way to making good their claim that they, and not the Irish Protestants, were the Irish nation. But they still had not defined their relationship with the British state, with the United Kingdom. And there was perhaps still hope that their growing consciousness of themselves as the Irish majority, the Irish people, might be in some way modified, perhaps even transcended.

Political developments in Great Britain and Ireland were mutually important. Thomas Davis and his followers wanted to create a new sense of Irishness through the fostering of Irish culture: literature, history, the arts, would all be pressed into service and, through them, Irishmen would discover a rich past, one that would give them self-confidence in a world dominated by the culture, history and language of England. Irishmen would place the nation above the individual, and the different kinds of Irish people could nourish themselves on a common culture. It was not clear where this common culture could be found, for the history of Ireland, at least since early modern times, was a story of division and strife. Nevertheless, Davis and his followers set out with confidence and commitment, publishing books, pamphlets and a newspaper – the *Nation* – to mould a new Ireland, an Ireland of the mind, an Ireland of the imagination.

But the creation of such an Ireland might have been, all unwittingly, helped by Peel's desire to give the Roman Catholic middle classes what they most desperately needed: a good university education. Peel wanted the Catholic to feel, as well as be, the equal of the Protestant, and he devised the policy of establishing 'Queen's Colleges' in Belfast, Cork and Galway, which would provide a non-denominational university, thus offering Catholics an alternative to the Protestant establishment of Trinity College Dublin. Here was an opportunity to institutionalize the new Ireland that Davis imagined; for now Catholic and Protestant alike would mix, learn and live together. Thus Young Ireland, and, initially, some Roman Catholic bishops and Catholic liberals supported the colleges. But O'Connell, with strong support from the anti-college hierarchy, strongly opposed them, revealing once again that, when his generally tolerant religious views conflicted with political necessities, he invariably chose the political path. Peel's government carried its university legislation and the colleges were established (though by 1852 Catholics were prohibited by their church from entering them, except for purely professional qualifications). Davis failed to overcome O'Connell's opposition and the gap between old and Young Ireland was painfully revealed in May 1845, when O'Connell reduced Davis to tears with his brutal accusation that Davis had implied that it was a 'crime to be a Catholic' (Boyce, 1991, pp. 165–6).

This controversy also revealed the danger to Catholic political solidarity from British government policies. Reform might divide the nationalist camp and it might, if acceptable, undermine the sense of grievance upon which O'Connell built his repeal movement. This was seen in Peel's Charitable Bequests Bill of 1844, which set up a new bequest board of thirteen, including five Catholics, to administer charitable donations and act as trustees for property used to maintain Catholic clergy and buildings. This new board would replace the exclusively Protestant body created in 1800. O'Connell and MacHale opposed the measure strongly (despite its obvious advantages for Catholics) because it might indeed drive a wedge into Catholic solidarity and make Catholics dependent on the British crown. MacHale also feared that for Catholics to associate with Protestants on the board might prove in some way contaminating. Three Catholic archbishops (Dublin, Armagh, and Down and Conor) were none the less gazetted as members. The British government was exuberant: they had at last split Catholic solidarity and given the lie to O'Connell's claim that he, and he alone, spoke for Catholic Ireland (Boyce, 1990, pp. 89–91).

Irish Protestants studied these developments with a lively interest. It was galling to see a British government – above all

25

a Conservative government – brush aside their claims that upon the Protestants, and upon them alone, depended the safety of the Union. Most Protestants were unmoved by the efforts of Davis and Young Ireland to create a new common culture (as of course were most Catholics). Majority Protestant fears were expressed by a young, energetic and able Protestant lawyer, Isaac Butt, who debated the issue of Ireland under the Union with O'Connell in the Dublin Corporation. Municipal reform had been another Protestant bulwark sacrificed to the Catholics on the altar of appeasement, and Butt had opposed it eloquently but unsuccessfully. Now, confronted with the Liberator, Butt made a superb defence of the status quo. Repeal was not a return to Grattan's parliament of 1782; and anyway, that parliamentary experiment had ended up in the chaos and bloodshed of 1798. Repeal would be to embark on a revolutionary course, because it meant entering on an 'untried and wild system of democracy'. Butt saw democracy as many Victorians did, as a danger to liberty and the whole constitutional system, given, in Ireland, a special twist through its association with Catholic political ambitions. If democracy meant playing the game by numbers, then it was a useful game for Catholics to play; whether or not they would respect the need to look after the minority in a democratic Ireland remained doubtful. Butt put his finger, then, on a vital aspect of the making of modern Irish politics: the connections established, purely fortuitously, between Catholic ambitions, democratic politics and – thanks to O'Connell – the general idea of 'liberty', even of liberalism (Butt, 1843, *passim*).

Protestants might find it difficult to prevail against such hosts, but they would try. In Ulster they could try with greater hope of success, for while the southern Protestant, Isaac Butt, must rely on the power of words and cling to the hope that Britain would stand firm – a dubious one – Ulster Protestants had strength through their northern preponderance. They could hope to make democracy work on their behalf; neither numbers nor liberty would frighten them. In Ulster terms the Repealer need not be out-argued; the Repealer could be repulsed. And his repulse in January 1841 brought together Church of Ireland man and Presbyterian in a common cause. Whatever their political and social distinctions, they could in time of crisis discover their common Protestantism. As Dr Henry Cooke, the Presbyterian leader of the demonstration against O'Connell, put it 'the Bible and its principles', combined with the acknowledgement of the benefits of the Union, and allied to 'the genii of Protestantism and Liberty, sitting inseparable in their power, while the genius of industry reclines at their feet' made Protestants of all sorts resolved to 'advance and secure the prosperity of our country' (Porter, 1871, pp. 412–13).

There were Protestants of a more conciliatory disposition who hoped to find a middle way between repeal and the seamless Union. An Ulster Liberal Protestant landlord, William Sharman Crawford, had, as early as the 1830s, produced a federal scheme for Ireland and Great Britain, involving an appropriate division of powers between the Irish and imperial governments. O'Connell declared against federalism but, by 1844, he was past the prime of his political career, looking like a democrat without a democracy to govern. In these circumstances, O'Connell looked on federalism with a more friendly eye, especially if it promised to undermine or soften Protestant opposition.

O'Connell's idea of a federal settlement was more advanced than the home-rule schemes of the later nineteenth century, since he envisaged a system of an imperial Parliament, along with two, coequal legislatures (British and Irish). The problem was that this would involve a full-scale reorganization, and probably a rewriting of the British constitution, which would hardly appeal to British public opinion. Moreover, O'Connell's shifting position on federalism opened him to the accusation that he was merely opportunistic, that he worked from no consistent nationalist principle. Young Ireland accused him of being a federalist or a repealer as it suited his book. O'Connell, lacking any widespread public enthusiasm for federalism, and without even the solace of the emergence of any federal sentiment in Ulster, could only retreat ignominiously and deny that he had ever intended to compromise the constitutional rights inherited from Grattan's Parliament (*NHI*, 1989, p. 191).

It was not only O'Connell, Young Ireland and the federalists who were in disarray by 1845. Peel's policy of taking the Irish Catholic firmly into the United Kingdom suffered a set-back when his intention of increasing the grant paid by the state to Maynooth (the training institution for Catholic clergy) aroused vociferous opposition, especially in England, where the cry of 'no popery' still had echoes of the Armada and the Inquisition. Peel prevailed, but the vulgarity of his opponents, and the more considered opposition of those who held that any state aid to a religious institution was wrong, damaged the concession, and limited its value. Once again it seemed that Irish Catholics could expect benefits from the Union only after a struggle, and one accompanied by harsh words, as they had first discovered in the emancipation campaign of 1828–9 (Boyce, 1990, pp. 91–2).

These political disagreements were soon to shrink in importance, compared with the economic and social catastrophe that engulfed rural Ireland. The partial failure of the potato crop in 1845 first provoked a crisis in British rather than Irish politics, as Peel used the occasion to repeal the corn laws, which were the very foundation of the protection of British agriculture against foreign imports of food. In June 1846 the Conservative party split and remained divided for two decades. This might have given O'Connell an opportunity for another round of Whig co-operation and the implementation of a further list of reforms (the franchise, the grand jury, municipal government and land-lord–tenant relations, a tax on absentee landlords and another push for denominational education). It also aroused the suspicion of Young Ireland, which rated reform well below the question of raising the level of national consciousness and national life. Once again the aspirations of the Catholic people of Ireland seemed to stand in the way of the creation of a nation of the mind, a community bound together by the Irish language, literature, and a sense of a great past, such as that enjoyed by the Greeks.

It was unfortunate for Young Ireland that it lost Thomas Davis, who died in September 1845, for Davis was essentially a moderate man when it came to politics, preferring to direct his energies into warning Irishmen of all persuasions that they had better seek reconciliation rather than conflict. Davis never solved the question of how that reconciliation might be achieved, for his version of Irish history was naïve: England was the problem, and Irishmen could evolve a common culture, once free of English influence. But at least he saw education, rather than war, as the best means of giving his fellow country-men their self-respect and a sense of genuine nationhood. Now, however, Young Ireland began to speak in more militant terms. And while their militancy was confined to words rather than deeds, it was enough to allow O'Connell to manoeuvre them on to his ground and then drive them from his movement. In January 1846 he drew up a resolution that all political action must be constitutional and Young Ireland responded by making the matter one of principle. John Mitchel, an Ulster Presbyter-ian of United Irishman views, agreed to the motion, but refused to assent to any ultimate rejection of the sword as a means of gaining Irish freedom. 'The men of '98 thought liberty worth some bloodletting.'

'What can this man's object be,' interposed O'Connell, 'He purports to be a man of peace, yet he preaches of war.' O'Con-nell insisted, as he put it, on 'drawing the line' between Young and old Ireland: 'I do not accept the services of any man who does not agree with me both in theory and in practice', and called for the 'ignominious expulsion' of any man who did not adhere to the association's rules. Young Ireland accepted the motion, but by the end of July 1846 they seceded (O'Hegarty, 1952, pp. 243–5). It might be said of them that they died of a theory, like the American Confederacy. The unlooked-for effect of this split was to weaken nationalist Ireland when the country was on the verge of a great famine.

3

The Famine, the Fenians and Gladstone, 1846–1870

If the popular image of early nineteenth-century England is one deeply influenced by contemporary pictures of children working in factories and coalmines, then the image of Ireland is one shaped by similar drawings, this time of rural children, but children in rags and poverty. Yet when William Makepeace Thackeray visited Ireland in 1842 he was indeed greeted everywhere he went by ragged people, especially children, but he noted that those he encountered had cheerful countenances and a generally friendly disposition. This may have been a fleeting impression and a misleading one, gathered by a bemused tourist, but perhaps it reflected the fact that the bulk of the population, though poor, had enough to eat, and was spared at least the worst kind of living conditions experienced by the urban poor in Great Britain (Thackeray, 1842, *passim*; *NHI*, 1989, pp. 108–12).

The Irish rural population had another advantage over the urban population: the potato, a cheap, wholesome and easily grown root. Yet there were signs that the population of Ireland was increasing to such an extent, and at such a rate, that its dependence on the potato might prove its nemesis, not its salvation. There was a crisis in 1816–17, when an unusually cold and wet summer caused serious damage to the crop. Hunger and desperation were, for the first time, brought to the attention of Dublin Castle. Sir Robert Peel's response was characteristically thorough, if a little tardy. He obtained from the government funds for relief measures amounting to some £37,000 (*NHI*, 1989, pp. 61–2).

The blight that struck the potato crop in 1845 was not at first a serious problem; it became one when it persisted for several years, destroying crops even as they were re-sown. No one could have anticipated such a sustained and widespread blight, and Ireland was soon in the grip of a crisis of unprecedented severity. The government was faced with several difficulties in dealing with the famine. There was an ingrained official caution about the extent of the problem, and even a scepticism about its gravity. This was followed by a realization that indeed the famine presented an unprecedented challenge to the state, but also a reluctance to commit the state and its resources on too large a scale, partly because of the economic orthodoxy of the day, partly because Ireland was rather far away and (like contemporary Scotland) deserved help – but not on the scale that her advocates, including many leading Protestants, called for. There was also an underlying feeling among some officials that Ireland, like Scotland, would ultimately benefit from the restructuring which the famine must bring about, that her antiquated social system would be replaced by a more modern, enduring one. This was the view held by Charles Trevelyan, assistant secretary to the Treasury, who in April 1846 believed that, by withholding too large a release of government food stocks, the Irish landlords would be forced to accept proper responsibility for providing relief (*NHI*, 1989, p. 279).

Peel was Prime Minister when the famine became an object of general attention. As early as October 1845 he was alerted to the disaster and his response was to use the occasion to repeal the corn laws and open the United Kingdom to free trade. This would not, of course, have any immediate palliative impact on Ireland, but Peel laid down a programme of relief, following the precedent of 1816–17. He set up a relief commission, and organized food depots and local committees to administer relief. When Peel fell from power in the summer of 1846 the Whig government inherited the second, more serious stage of famine. They were reluctant to import more food, partly because private traders were angered at the state's unwarranted interference in the market. Charles Trevelyan nonetheless did import food, despite its rising price, but he was conscious of the fact that Europe as a whole was experiencing varying degrees of distress, and he was anxious not to overburden the 'English and Scotch landowners' with the cost of feeding Ireland – thus unwittingly denying the central concept of Great Britain and Ireland as a *United* Kingdom (Daly, 1986, p. 72).

Yet he realized – as all government officials came to realize – that Ireland must be fed. No one wanted Ireland to starve, but the hope of letting the free market cope, so that food prices would fall, was frustrated and prices rose in 1847. The government did not leave all to the market, for it provided direct relief in the form of public works. These would have had the advantage of providing labour, thus enabling people to earn money to buy food, and also the accomplishment of useful tasks, such as land drainage and road improvements. But the severe crisis of the winter of 1846–7 quickly made these measures obsolete. Food prices increased and the administration of public works on such a large scale proved difficult and, in the more remote areas, impossible. And anyway many people were simply not able-bodied enough to perform the manual tasks involved.

Instead of relief work the state now set up soup-kitchens. These were to be administered by local committees and a new commission was established to oversee relief. However, the cost of the food, after a start-up grant, was thrown on the local poor rates. Soup-kitchens were in widespread use by the summer of 1847, and at the height of the famine over three million people were seeking relief in them and in workhouses.

The great famine accelerated existing social trends rather than bringing about a total transformation of the existing structure. Precise figures of the number who died as a direct result of the famine are hard to obtain: a modern calculation (which includes all deaths for the years 1846–51) puts the number at about one million. Some areas were more severely ravaged by famine. Connaught suffered most, Ulster least, but there were regional variations even within these areas. South Ulster was more stricken than north-east Ulster. Mortality figures must also take into account a cholera epidemic which, independently of the famine, spread through certain areas of Ulster, notably Belfast. The famine was followed by a dramatic fall in the birth rate, an enormous decrease in the number of people for whom Irish was their first language, and a rapid and irreversible decline in the poorer sectors of rural society, the cottiers and labourers, who were swept away by death and emigration. This resulted in a consolidation of farms, a decrease in the number of smallholdings (again, with important regional variations) and the beginnings of the emergence of the central, important, social group in modern Irish history: the tenant farmer with a medium to large holding, who had escaped the worst of the famine, but who saw it change his economic and ultimately political prospects. In 1845 36 per cent of farms were of over fifteen acres; by 1851 the figure was 51 per cent. The percentage of holdings of under five acres fell from 24 per cent to 15 per cent (Daly, 1986, p. 120).

But statistics do not tell the full story. Irish society, at least its rural poor, underwent a trauma. Contemporary witnesses bore out the horror of disease, starvation and the demoralization of those least able to defend themselves against want. And, while this was not of immediate political significance (since the dying and the emigrant have other preoccupations) yet it was to provide material for grievances which a later generation would raise. There were questions about the integrity of the British government, its willingness or unwillingness to act; questions about landlords who evicted tenants at the height of the famine; questions about the most wounding assertion of all: that Protestants had sought to use the occasion to proselytize Catholics through offering food for conversion – 'souperism'.

Some of these accusations do not stand up to modern investigation. No British government wanted the Irish people to starve: there was no desire for, or even a notion of genocide. Much of the failure of the government's measures was because of its slowness to grasp the scale of the disaster (and, even more important, to anticipate its recurrence) and the difficulty of administering relief in the more remote areas, which had poor communications. Yet there was undoubtedly an impatience with

Ireland, which Isaac Butt, the Protestant, Conservative lawyer, complained about when he declared that

> all measures that have yet been proposed by ministers are passed on the principle that Ireland herself must bear the burden of this unprecedented visitation; while the aid that imperial credit might afford her for the development of her own resources is either altogether refused, or given in so niggardly and procrastinating a dole that it becomes useless (Butt, 1847, p. 55).

This impatience arose in Britain from the response to Irish politics of the previous two decades or more. Here was a country whose political leaders, in particular Daniel O'Connell, had spared England no criticism and no embarrassment. Now it was coming to England, cap in hand, for help. This feeling reinforced the general prejudice about the link between the Irish character and unreasonable political behaviour. But no government – not even Lord John Russell's Liberal government which replaced Sir Robert Peel's Conservative administration in the summer of 1846 – could ignore the mounting evidence of disaster. England would wearily shoulder what she regarded as the 'Irish burden' yet again. And the British public, for its part, made a most generous charitable response.

The British government was slow to take fuller responsibility for the famine relief because it believed that the main burden should be carried by Irish landed property. Landlords had to collect rent and yet, with diminished resources, meet heavy poor rates and provide employment. Landlords did not starve, but many did go bankrupt. And some, faced with an economic crisis that they could not manage, felt that they had no choice but to evict tenants in the hope that, by intensifying human misery now, they might modernize their estate management in the near future, with happier consequences for all concerned. Smaller tenants were the least likely to pay their rent and the most likely to need famine relief. The number of evictions appears large: 6,026 in 1847; 9,657 in 1848; 16,686 in 1849; 19,949 in 1850. Yet the total number of evictions by 1850 constituted only 2.5 per cent of the total number of agricultural holdings (Daly, 1986, p. 110). Many landlords chose to lose money or fall into debt, rather than evict.

Souperism – the pressurizing of Roman Catholics to convert through the offer of food – was practised, but on a small scale; and against this must be set the self-sacrifice of many Protestant clergy, who co-operated wholeheartedly with their Roman Catholic fellow-Christians to alleviate suffering, often at the cost of their own lives. But the image of souperism revealed how even a natural catastrophe could be reduced to political and sectarian terms in a country with no settled political condition. And the poor who fled to Great Britain and America in the famine years were to provide a retrospective condemnation of Britain for its alleged 'murder' of the Irish people, as well as a source of money for Irish nationalist movements, revolutionary and constitutional. Yet, even here, it is important not to overstate the impact of the famine. There were plenty of real, present grievances for nationalists to exploit in Ireland, besides the memories and images of famine. The Irish abroad might cling to the memory of a lost Eden; the Irish at home had more immediate concerns and founded their politics less on memories of famine victims (who were in any case the poorest and least regarded part of the population) than on expectations and fears of what lay in store for those who now lived in Ireland. The tenant farmers of Ireland cared little for famine victims, other than as a propaganda weapon and a dire warning; they were determined not to go the same way, and even hoped that they might better themselves in time to come.

These hopes had to be advanced in the context of the Union; these fears shaped their attitude towards the Union and how best it might be exploited or even, perhaps, modified. They were certainly unaffected by the attempt made in 1848 by the Young Irelanders to rebel and throw off British rule. When O'Connell broke with Young Ireland in July 1846 his critics formed an 'Irish Confederation' to put an end to sectarian divisions by abandoning the 'ultra-Catholic' and 'ultra-democratic' politics of O'Connell (*NHI*, 1989, p. 361). This characterization of O'Connellism is important, for it expressed what was indeed the case then and would become more significantly true in the later nineteenth century. The nationalism that aspired to be secular and liberal was always a minority sentiment, and was indeed often a revolutionary and anti-democratic movement and ideology. Majority nationalism was democratic, but (as Young Ireland alleged) was also Roman Catholic in character. Therefore, neither the revolutionary nationalism of Young Ireland, nor the democratic nationalism of old Ireland held much attraction for the Protestants as a whole. Secular nationalism aimed at breaking the link between Great Britain and Ireland upon which Protestants felt their prosperity and survival depended. Democratic nationalism might tolerate certain links between Britain and Ireland, but on terms laid down by a permanent Catholic majority. Frustration at government policy during the famine and objections to government belief that Irish property must bear the burden of relief brought about an interest on the part of some Protestant Conservatives in cooperating with the repeal and Young Ireland movements to attack government policy. But this was only a temporary excursion into deep and dangerous political waters.

Young Ireland, having broken with O'Connell, found itself edging towards a revolutionary gesture. This was not only because of its anger and frustration at what it regarded as government passivity in the face of famine. It was also a result of the excitement generated by events in Europe, and especially France. 'It is not on foreign aid the people of Ireland should depend but on themselves,' declared the young, Protestant William Smith O'Brien at a meeting of the Irish Confederation in March 1848. But, he added, 'if we did look for French sympathy, there are some of the members of the present provisional government in France who have expressed their willingness to extend it to us (cheers)' (*United Irishman*, 11 March 1848).

It was at this stage in her history that Ireland lost the services of its greatest political figure of the nineteenth century. Daniel O'Connell played no significant part in the politics of the famine years. Indeed, ever since his imprisonment in 1843, he suffered a gradual but inexorable political eclipse. He could maintain his authority in the majority nationalist movement for repeal, but his power to arouse Ireland, to win famous victories, was gone, and his determination to drive Young Ireland out of his movement was a symptom of his frustration, not of his power. He fell ill, and died on his way to Rome in May 1847. Catholic Ireland had much to thank him for, and his was essentially a moderating role in an era of social and political upheaval. Yet his populist style, his frequently alarming language (though intended to diffuse rather than arouse passions) provoked fear in Irish Protestants and confirmed their suspicion that there would be no easy place for them in an O'Connellite Ireland.

1848 was a good year for would-be revolutionaries. 'Up with the barricades, and invoke the God of battles', proclaimed the *Nation* (O'Hegarty, 1952, p. 367). John Mitchel looked to his famous ancestors of 1798, and held that 'moral force must be set aside for the one and all sufficient remedy, the edge of the sword' (Mitchel, n.d., p. 24). In August 1848 Young Ireland raised its revolt, which turned out to be a series of (sometimes farcical) skirmishes with the police, which Mitchel blamed in retrospect on Irishmen's lack of training in the use of weapons: 'the sight of clean steel, and of blood smoking hot, must become familiar to men, boys, women' (Ibid., pp. 143–4). But Ireland was spared this Armageddon, and the leaders of the rebellion were arrested and transported. There were no executions and no martyrs, but later generations of revolutionaries looked to Mitchel's words to justify direct action and the frustration of majority will.

Meanwhile the British government had to cope with the aftermath of famine. Whatever the desire of governments to forget about Ireland – an ungrateful country which insisted upon electing repealers even as Britain put bread in her mouth – the famine pushed the state into approaching, however reluctantly, the great central question of nineteenth-century Ireland: the land. This question was not seen only, or even mainly, in economic terms. It was soon linked with questions of history, politics and the dismantling of the Protestant landlord ascendancy, the ascendancy that claimed it was the only sure bulwark of the Union in Ireland. But in 1848 the first tentative steps were forced on the government by the bankruptcy of many landlords and the immediate need to sell large acreages of landed property, which, it was hoped, would be bought by new, modern and efficient owners who would make the landed system pay again. The Encumbered Estates Act of 1849 (replacing an earlier measure of 1848) created a court empowered to sell estates on application from owners or from those who had a legal claim upon the estate (e.g. a mortgage). This would have the effect of lowering land values by putting more property on the market and, in turn, would devalue the property of those landlords who were hoping to hold on to their lands. But the purchasers of land were not, as the act intended, modernizing English and Scottish proprietors. They were local men, mainly from landed and professional backgrounds, and they were buying at a time when the production of profits, and tighter estate management, were regarded as the only criteria for making a land system work. (*NHI*, 1989, pp. 348–9).

These circumstances would naturally have an effect on land-lord–tenant relations. There were already voices calling for a different land system altogether, one which would retain the idea of land as private property, but which would transfer that right to the tenant. The chief propagandist of this view was James Fintan Lalor, who declared that the lands 'were owned by the conquering race, or by traitors to the conquered race. They were *occupied* by the native people, or by settlers who had mingled and merged.' The land could be reconquered through the refusal to pay rent and arrears, and by resistance to government. There must be a right to private property, 'the right of a man to possess, enjoy, and transfer, the substance and use of whatever he has *himself* created'. Lalor hoped that this might be achieved through direct action, a rent strike, or perhaps even revolution as in 1848 (Marlowe, 1918, pp. 84–98). But after the famine the tenant farmers, on whom he placed his reliance for this change in property holding, were beginning to emerge as a political and economic pressure group of a non-revolutionary but none the less influential kind. The 1850 franchise reform act gave the vote to thousands of farmers in every county in Ireland, raising the county electorate from 60,597 in 1832 to 135,245 in 1851–2. The farmers who got the vote were tenants who held land valued at twelve pounds or more – about twelve acres of good land – and thus formed a group with middling and large farms (*NHI*, 1989, pp. 382–3, 400). Farmers had an incentive to act collectively after 1850. Prices fell after the temporary rise in 1847, and Ulster gave the lead in collective action. Here tenant farmers enjoyed what was known as the 'Ulster custom', which enabled the tenant to ask an incoming purchaser for a payment of money in return for his enjoyment of a settled tenancy: a kind of goodwill payment which, however, landlords might wish to interfere with. Many Ulster farmers were Presbyterians, and fully disposed to stand up for their rights against their Church of Ireland landlords. They would not of course challenge the political hegemony of their landlords, but they were interested enough in making common cause with tenants elsewhere to participate in the 'League of North and South', founded in 1850 to advance the interests of the farmers of Ireland.

There were many obstacles to Catholic–Presbyterian co-operation, not least the growing influence of both the Catholic Church and evangelical Protestantism, with its emphasis on the imperative necessity to save souls and spread the word of God throughout Ireland. There was also the problem of devising a dividing line between what might be regarded as the economic interests of tenants, which could be held in common, and the political implications of their actions, which might prove divisive. This was soon evident. Charles Gavan Duffy, a Young Irelander who re-founded the *Nation* in 1850, gave a lead; other newspaper proprietors of a liberal disposition followed. They sought to enlist the support of Irish Members of Parliament, but it was not until the general election of 1852 that the League managed to win the pledged support of forty-two members who promised to press for a bill on tenant right. But the success was undermined by the fact that, despite the strength of Presbyterian tenant farmers in Ulster, few tenant-right candidates were successful in the north. The old fear of Catholic politics was coming to the fore. Irish Protestant Conservatives made a determined counter-attack, playing the Catholic card, and concentrating upon the Presbyterian tenants' fear of a Roman Catholic resurgence.

In any event, the policy of independent opposition was difficult to operate in the Westminster politics of the mid-nineteenth century, where parties were loose associations of members under a very imperfect discipline. There was also a natural affinity between members of the independent party and the British Liberals, who had, moreover, political patronage at their disposal. Two leading members of the independent party, William Keogh and John Sadleir, defected to government posts. In Ireland, the Roman Catholic church was more favourably inclined towards the Irish Liberals than towards the independents. By 1855 Gavan Duffy, despairing of influencing political events, resigned his seat and emigrated to Australia. No tenants rights bill came within even the most remote prospect of success in Parliament (Boyce, 1990, pp. 126–30).

By the 1850s Irish politics seemed to be settling down into a comfortable enough pattern, or at least a pattern comfortable to the establishment. Landlords used their influence to secure the votes of their tenants and interest, rather than political principles, oiled the wheels. The wheels of British politics even turned a little in favour of Roman Catholics, as Lord Derby's government, formed in 1858, was a minority one which, seeking as much support as possible, made many useful concessions to Catholics. But even as this comfortable world seemed assured for decades to come, a new organization was formed in Ireland to take advantage of the Anglo-French tension that obsessed the United Kingdom in the late 1850s: the Fenian Brotherhood.

It is still hard to disentangle the myth and reality of Fenianism. It has been subjected to rigorous modern historical examination, yet its strength, its motives, its ideology and the seriousness of its threat to the state remain open to debate. The Brotherhood was founded by James Stephens in Dublin in 1858 and it owed some of its character to Young Ireland, especially its more romantic and literary aspects. Like Young Ireland, and indeed the United Irishmen, the Fenians looked to foreign, especially French, assistance. But it developed two characteristics that marked it off from these earlier movements. It had

40

an agrarian policy, which held that the 'land is the property of the people', and not the 'inheritance of the privileged class'. Thus it should be 'parcelled out by the state, on such terms as are most conducive to protect and to promote the interests of all'. A 'peasant propriety' was needed (*Irish People*, 30 July 1864). The Fenians were relentless critics of landlords, but also of rich and middling farmers, and especially farmers who turned their lands over to grazing, thus depriving the poorer rural people of a living. They moved beyond the middle-class urban radicals of 1798 and the romantics of 1848, and enlisted support from the young, from towns and cities, from Irishmen in the British army and from the Irish who lived in Great Britain. An index of names of suspected Fenians, compiled in Dublin Castle in 1866–71, included a national school teacher, a drapery shop worker, a clerk of works, a drapers' assistant, a newspaper editor, a newsagent, a draper, a shopkeeper, a private of the 84th Foot, a cooper, a medical student, an assurance society agent, a shoemaker and a mercantile clerk (SPOI, Irish Crimes Records 1866–72, VIIIB, W.P. 3/6, 7).

This was a motley collection. If its members had anything in common it was their distinction from the core group in rural Ireland: the up-and-coming tenant farmers. This was one grievous weakness; another was their inability to come to terms with the Roman Catholic Church in Ireland. Fenians were not as hostile to the Church as later commentators liked to believe: 'We never intended a word against the priests as ministers of religion,' wrote the Fenian Charles Kickham. 'We did not hold that priests should be excluded from politics, but that as politicians they should be heeded no more than other men, but rather less, as they have mostly shown themselves very bad politicians.' This was clearly not a stand against the priest in politics in any principled, let alone anticlerical fashion (O'Leary, 1896, II, p. 33). And despite the hostility of the hierarchy, which feared that Ireland was suffering from the Godless revolutionary fever of the continent, many lower clergy sympathized with Fenians. Thus the Brotherhood had the worst of both worlds: it neither broke sufficiently with the Church in a way that would make its secular nationalism a reality; nor did it accommodate itself to the Church in order to gain the support, which was essential if Fenianism was to capture the minds of the Irish majority.

Fenians hardly seemed a serious threat. They wrote much, debated a great deal, held social outings and quarrelled among themselves. They were lucky, however, in that the 1850s and 1860s were a good time in which to be Irish and Catholic. Roman Catholics from Ireland were cutting a dash in Europe, fighting in Italy (for France against the Austrians) and, in 1861, showing their military prowess in the American Civil War. They staged a significant propaganda coup when they transported the body of a Young Irelander, Terence Bellew MacManus, from America to Dublin, and gave him a spectacular funeral in November 1861 (Comerford, 1985, pp. 74–80). But it was hard to turn these displays of pride and sentiment into enduring political reality; even a large demonstration, like the one at the Mac-Manus funeral, was not necessarily a sign that the nation supported revolution. In 1867 the Fenians at last struck their blow for freedom. It turned out to be sporadic, weakly supported and easily suppressed. Fenian outrages in Great Britain, including an attack on Chester Castle, were no more successful, but they did have a profound impact on British public opinion. The immediate British response gave the Fenians a much-needed boost to their prestige. In November 1869 three Fenians were hanged for their part in a rescue attempt that resulted in shooting dead a policeman in Manchester. The three were soon celebrated in verse and song and became known as the 'Manchester Martyrs'; annual pilgrimages were held in Ireland to commemorate them. This, of course, further strengthened the connection between nationalism and Catholicism, despite the formal condemnation of Fenianism by the Pope in 1870. But then 'love of country' and 'love of religion', as Cardinal Paul Cullen observed, were by now inseparable in Ireland anyway (Mac Suibhne, 1961, pp. 408–10).

Irish Roman Catholics were helped by the Fenian episode into a rediscovered self-consciousness, but it remained to be seen whether or not this could be turned to political account. That it was so turned was the consequence of developments

42

beyond Ireland, as the whole British Isles were on the verge of a new political era, one in which popular, if not yet democratic politics, were emerging at the centre of the political stage. Local groups and communities were stirring, Nonconformists in Wales, Presbyterians in Scotland, Roman Catholics in Ireland, and new voices were being given effect, not least through the efforts of William Ewart Gladstone, who was soon to be the master of the politics of the Celtic Fringe.

The British government was deeply alarmed by developments in Ireland after the abortive rising of 1867, especially by the campaign, launched in July 1869, for an amnesty to be granted to Fenian prisoners. Gladstone was obliged to sanction coercion in order to maintain law and order, but he had an unswerving faith in the power of public opinion, properly organized and given moral leadership. He set himself to tap this resource in Ireland and offer it the voice it could not find for itself. Liberal Ireland would cease to be the happy hunting-ground of the place-seeker; it would be the embodiment of Catholic – and of course Presbyterian – hopes. Ireland would participate in the great awakening of the Celtic lands.

Gladstone took advantage of the fears generated in Britain by Fenianism to launch a crusade for the government of Ireland by what he called 'Irish ideas'. His first choice for reform was the Church of Ireland, for here was a good cause, a moral cause, and one, moreover, that would unite British nonconformity behind the Liberal party. Irish Catholics and Irish Presbyterians would not stand up and defend a Church to which they did not subscribe. Irish Protestants watched in consternation as a British prime minister attacked what they regarded as the very root of the true religion in Ireland, one of the foundation stones of the Union: the established state Church of Ireland.

British Conservatives fought a weak rearguard action, for they could not bring themselves to defend to the death what was hardly, in rational terms, defensible. The general election of 1868 revealed the contours of the new political map in Ireland. Liberals won seats, not only in southern constituencies, but in Ulster as well. Gladstone gathered sixty-six Irish followers, the vast majority of Catholic or Presbyterian faith. He pressed ahead with the disestablishment and disendowment of the Church of Ireland, and in July 1869 his bill became law. The Church's property was given over to be administered by a Church Temporalities Commission, and half its value was returned to the Church for the support of the clergy; the other half was raised to compensate the Presbyterians for the loss of their state grant and Maynooth for the loss of its parliamentary grant.

It seemed, then, that by 1869 Catholic and Presbyterian Ireland would be Liberal Ireland, and Liberal Ireland would be for Gladstone. This prospect was enhanced by Gladstone's next excursion into Irish problems. In 1870 he tackled the second branch of the Irish difficulty, as he saw it: the land issue. Gladstone ventured into the thorny area of landlord–tenant relations, giving legal force to the 'Ulster custom' wherever it was already found and seeking to create legal equivalents of this custom where it did not already exist. He also gave tenants compensations for improvements made in their holdings and compensation for disturbance when they were evicted for causes other than the non-payment of rent. The central weakness of this measure was that the compensation was not nearly high enough to enable an evicted tenant to purchase another farm, and insolvent tenants were, in the nature of things, a more volatile and anxious set of people than those who were comfortably off. Their vulnerability to economic recession was soon to be demonstrated, with dramatic effect, in 1879 (*NHI*, 1989, pp. 757–8).

Even as Gladstone rode high in Ireland, his position was already weakening. The disappointment over his 1870 Land Act was soon felt and his notion of the government of Ireland by Irish ideas was about to be given a new challenge. In May 1870 the Home Government Association was founded to explore the possibility of combining Protestants and Catholics in a movement aimed at giving Ireland a federal government within the United Kingdom. These twin issues, as they were soon to become, of land and home rule dominated Irish politics from 1870 until the outbreak of the Great War.

4

The Politics of Home Rule, 1870–1893

When Isaac Butt explored the possibility of founding a new Irish political party in 1870 he had high hopes of gathering within its ranks Protestants and Dissenters, as well as Catholics. He himself had made a political migration, from the politics of Conservatism and unbending defence of the Union to a concern for the Irish economy in the famine years and now to a belief that only with her own federal institutions could Ireland settle down to become a prosperous and contented member of the United Kingdom. Irish Conservatives, dismayed at Britain's apostasy in 1869 and her attack on landlord rights in 1870, were in a restive mood, tempted briefly to show England that they would stand on their own feet. The committee formed in May 1870 to work for home government included twenty-eight Protestant Conservatives, ten Liberals (two of whom were Presbyterians), seven Catholics, one man of unknown persuasion (a rare phenomenon), seventeen constitutional nationalists (five Protestant and twelve Catholics) and six Fenians or Fenian associates (all Catholics). The weight of Conservative influence was shown in the demand for 'a vigorous, healthy, united lay public opinion' which should, specifically, reject Catholic claims for educational reform. But as the association expanded and became more popular, Conservative influence declined (Corish, 1967, pp. 48–9).

The reason was that the new association soon provided an

obvious forum for Catholic, rather than Protestant, grievances. Gladstone's refusal to free any more Fenian prisoners, in October 1869, caused resentment in the Amnesty Association. In November 1869 a convicted felon, O'Donovan Rossa, was elected to a parliamentary seat in Tipperary. Gladstone's Land Act proved less helpful to tenants than had been expected. When the Home Government Association first met publicly in September 1870, Protestant Conservatives had lost control. In 1873 Gladstone further forfeited Roman Catholic support and goodwill when his education bill failed to satisfy the Roman Catholic hierarchy. Irish Liberals voted against the government. Large numbers of priests began to announce their support for home government (or home rule, as it was called from November 1873). The measure of home rulers' success was discovered when in January 1874 Gladstone dissolved Parliament. Ireland returned fifty-nine home rulers, together with a mixed bag of Whigs and Liberals. Since a Tory government was now in power, the Irish opposition found itself a distinct group and avoided the usual fate of drifting towards the Liberal camp. But by now Irish Protestants were, for the most part, regarding the home rulers as a Catholic party for the Catholic people of Ireland, and not, as Butt originally intended, an Irish party for all the people of Ireland.

Butt has often been characterized as an ineffective leader of the home-rule party. Certainly he was a firm believer in the British parliamentary system, but he was determined to take parliamentary time for Irish measures and put forward legislative proposals. He was also able to demonstrate the central proposition upon which home rule was based: that the Westminster Parliament had neither the time nor the expertise to govern Ireland effectively. But from 1875 a small group of his followers sought to exploit the congestion of parliamentary business through making lengthy speeches and deliberately wasting time. This ginger group was led by Joseph Biggar and a newcomer to the house, Charles Stewart Parnell, the member for Meath. Their tactics were no more than irritating, but they aroused interest in nationalist Ireland, which liked to see the 'Saxon Parliament' put at a disadvantage. Parnell exploited this in May

46

1877 by writing an open letter to Butt (who had criticized the 'obstructionist' tactics), explaining why he could not obey his leader, because to comply would leave the British political elite in command of the field, to the eternal disadvantage of Ireland (Thornley, 1964, pp. 322–7).

Parnell was playing for support among the more radical elements in Irish nationalism. He cultivated the Irish in Great Britain, as he was soon to cultivate those in America. In 1876 he gained a moment of notoriety when he declared that the 'Manchester Martyrs' were not, as Sir Michael Hicks Beach called them, 'Manchester murderers'. In August 1877 he was elected president of the Home Rule Confederation of Great Britain, an organization whose nationalism was more advanced than that of many Irish people in Ireland. In March 1878, in London, he secretly met with Fenian leaders to discuss mutual co-operation, though in this meeting he was cautious, showing himself 'a listener rather than a talker' (Moody, 1981, pp. 205–6).

These initiatives made him a man to watch, but Parnell was not yet a serious contender for the leadership of the parliamentary party. His career, and the shape of nationalist politics, were given a new direction by events that lay outside the realm of party politics or even traditional Fenian conspiracies. A new kind of revolution was brewing. In 1878 rural depression threatened to plunge Ireland, and especially the west of Ireland, into yet another crisis, perhaps even another 'black '47'. This was never likely, but the depression was severe enough to provoke despair among the less solvent tenant farmers and even to cause concern among those who had done well for themselves since 1850. The new crisis differed from past downturns, including the depression of 1860–3, in that this time it occasioned a popular and well organized movement in the west of Ireland. This was entirely the work of local activists: James Daly, a newspaper editor; Matthew Harris, a builder; and James J. Louden, a barrister and farmer, who called a meeting at Irishtown with local Fenian help (Comerford, 1985, pp. 227–9).

Parnell was aware of the possibilities of the new crisis, and between March and June 1879 he negotiated with Michael

Davitt, a Fenian and agrarian radical, and John Devoy, a prominent Irish American Fenian, to clear the ground for co-operation. This was to be based on Parnell's promise of support for a land agitation campaign in return for Fenian help, and Parnell undertook to lead the more advanced home rulers in the direction of a national legislature for Ireland, less clearly defined than Butt's federal scheme, but more in tune with the kind of propaganda put out by home rulers in the country and in the press, which emphasized the idea of 'Ireland a nation', coming into her own and winning freedom from the Saxon Parliament (Bew, 1978, p. 51).

Parnell attended an agrarian meeting in Westport, County Mayo, in June 1879, but he was still on the sidelines and played no part in the process by which the Land League was formed between June and August 1879. However, he showed once again that he was prepared to take risks, and even incur the displeasure of the Roman Catholic Church, anxious, as always, lest the agrarian agitation spread 'communistic' ideas. In October 1879 Parnell at last seized the initiative, calling a meeting in Dublin to consider the agrarian crisis and to put the Land League on a nationwide basis. Parnell, at Davitt's instigation, became president of the Land League, though he did not approve of Davitt's policy of land nationalization. Isaac Butt's death in May 1879 did not immediately give Parnell his opportunity to assume the leadership of the home-rule movement. Butt was replaced by William Shaw, a Protestant barrister and a moderate – and rather dull – man. In May 1880 Parnell at last felt strong enough to challenge Shaw for the leadership and won by 23 votes to 18. But the party was weakened by this struggle, and Parnell was left as leader of a small following of MPs, apparently of no significance in British politics. Parnell's following increased as his supporters won by-elections, encouraging conversions and those who saw the way the wind was blowing. But Parnell was still in no position to play any significant role in the Parliament where, in the end, power was located and Ireland's fate decided.

Parnell had his popular following in Ireland, and the Land League agitation assured him of a base, but it was a difficult one to exploit. Agrarian violence incurred the displeasure of the Roman Catholic hierarchy and Parnell was, after all, a Protestant and so especially vulnerable to their criticism. Moreover, he was very much aware of the fragile nature of the apparently solid Land League. Tenant farmers in Ireland were by no means alike in wealth and prospects. The poorer farmers of the west were in more serious circumstances than wealthier farmers in, say, County Cork, and the Presbyterian farmers of Ulster, while sharing many of the aspirations of the Land League, were anxious lest the agitation turn against landlords as Protestants. But he believed that land agitation could be directed into a general nationalist demand, into a demand for home rule. The popular ballads of the 'land war' pointed the way:

We care not for the agent, nor do we care for those
Who come upon us to distrain – we pay them back in
    blows,
And when hopeless, helpless, ruined, these landlords
    vile shall roam,
We'll hunt and hound them from the roofs they've
    held so long as home.

                                        (Zimmerman, 1966, p. 60)

The rightful owners of the land would soon become the rulers of their own country (Bew, 1978, p. 59).

Parnell was himself a landlord, though an unorthodox one, in that he placed his faith in the economic future of Ireland in industrial, not agrarian development. But he knew that the only way to save the landlords was to remove them from the line of fire: a settlement of the land question would enable the gentry to settle down among the people and perhaps even give them leadership again (Bew, 1980, pp. 61–2). And he was careful to link land with home rule, for in his view they were inseparable. He would continue his efforts, he said in 1880, 'until the tenant farmer is forced from the grinding tyranny of his landlord – until Ireland obtains the restoration of her ancient parliament' (*Connaught Telegraph*, 17 April 1880).

49

Parnell's essentially conservative ideas did not sit easily with his Fenian associations, but he was prepared to talk in vague terms of an Irish legislature (which appeared much more ambitious than it really was) and he was also prepared to let Fenians and Irish Americans believe that he was a separatist if that was what suited their book. But he wanted an end to the land agitation, not least because it stood in the way of what any would-be nationalist leader needed: the full and unreserved co-operation of the Roman Catholic hierarchy. Thus the policy of the British government was of lively interest to him. And Gladstone, though he had to use coercion to restore order to disturbed areas of Ireland, was ready to embark on another legislative experiment to appease the legitimate fears of the tenant farmers. Gladstone's Land Act of 1881 set up land courts to fix 'judicial rents' on application from either landlord or tenant, and this recognized the permanent interest of the tenant in his farm. Parnell, unlike Davitt, did not denounce the act, but asked for modifications to help tenants already in arrears and leaseholders so far excluded from any benefit. The Irish chief secretary, W. E. Forster, interpreted this as opposition to the act, and Parnell was arrested and imprisoned in Kilmainham Jail in October 1881.

The increase in agrarian violence that followed could only end in stalemate. The League was curtailed by the police and law courts and it was losing its coherence, as different regions reacted in their own way to the land act and to the government's legal action against the League. Yet the League could not be broken by coercion alone, and Gladstone, for his part, sought a compromise with Parnell, with whose help, he believed, he could restore peace to Ireland. Gladstone and Parnell reached agreement in May 1882. Parnell would be released from imprisonment, coercion would be relaxed and the land act amended. Parnell would do his utmost to win over tenants' support for the land act in its new form.

The so-called Kilmainham Treaty was not altogether popular in Ireland. Agrarian radicals denounced it as a compromise of their basic princiPlees, though most farmers would have been happy to enjoy its advantages. But the possibility of its creating a new era in Ireland – whether remote or not – was destroyed when the newly appointed chief secretary for Ireland, Lord Frederick Cavendish, and his under-secretary, T. H. Burke, were brutally murdered on 6 May by a secret society, the 'Invincibles'. Parnell nearly left politics over the atrocity, but he was persuaded to stay, and in the end matters turned out to his advantage, for his opposition to the coercion legislation that inevitably followed the murders rehabilitated his reputation in nationalist Ireland. Now he moved to build a new movement on the ruins of the Land League: a 'National League', founded in October 1882, incorporating the Land League but placing home rule in the forefront of its policy. Nevertheless, Parnell had not yet recovered the position he held in 1882, when he and Gladstone concluded the Kilmainham Treaty. He was regarded as of no political influence in Parliament, however much he might stand in for 'Captain Moonlight' in Irish rural areas.

Parnell was, however, on the verge of the breakthrough that changed not only nationalist politics but British politics as well. He owed this to the franchise reforms which the Liberal government was contemplating in 1884, and to a growing mood that something should be done to alleviate the Irish problem. Gladstone was aware of the danger that franchise reform would give seats to the home-rule party. But, as he wrote to Lord Hartington in December 1883, 'to withhold franchises from Ireland while giving them to England and Scotland, and to proclaim the principle of an unequal Union, is the greatest blow that can be struck by any human power at the Act of Union.' He calculated that nationalists would take twenty-five seats from the Liberals in Ireland and would increase their representation from forty to nearly eighty members (Matthew, 1990, pp. 87, 192). In June 1885 a Conservative caretaker government under Lord Salisbury took office, following a Tory and Irish voting combination which turned Gladstone out, and held power until elections could be held under the new franchise. Salisbury's government immediately suspended coercion in Ireland and introduced a land bill (later known as the Ashbourne Act) which provided for the tenant the whole sum of money needed to buy

51

his land, to be repaid at 4 per cent interest over forty-nine years. This turned out to be such a popular measure that within five years the funds set aside were exhausted. The Conservatives even seemed tempted by the idea of a federal settlement for Ireland, and the viceroy, Lord Carnarvon, exchanged ideas about Irish self-government with Parnell.

In December 1885 Gladstone's predictions about the impact of franchise reform on Ireland were realized. Parnell won eighty-five Irish seats in the general election, plus one in Liverpool. The Liberals won 335 seats, the Conservatives 249, and the difference between the two exactly equalled Parnell's following. But this was not as powerful a position as it first appeared. Parnell could keep either party out, but he could only put in the Liberals. All his efforts to induce Gladstone to reveal his plans for Ireland failed, and Gladstone, though he acknowledged that Parnell could claim to speak for the Irish democracy, had no intention of making a premature move. Yet he had come to embrace the concept that was to dominate Anglo-Irish relations for the next thirty years: home rule for Ireland.

Gladstone's move towards home rule was no sudden, blinding conversion, but neither was it a kind of linear progression, with home rule following inevitably from disestablishment of the Church of Ireland and land reform. Gladstone, like any politician, had many preoccupations; Ireland was but one among many imperial and domestic affairs. But two perceptions drove him towards home rule: he believed in the power of moral judgement in politics (though he was not above squaring it with political necessities as well) and he believed that public opinion must be the stuff of political life – public opinion properly led, possessing a strong affection for the law and public institutions. Ireland was a moral problem; coercion was not, ultimately, the answer. Moreover, Irish public opinion lacked what Scottish opinion enjoyed: a close association with governing structures and the law. Gladstone assumed too that the British Parliament was a place where political conflicts could be resolved. The resolution of the Irish conflict through home rule was, he came to believe, essential, and he could cite precedents in both the empire and Europe: Canada and Norway pointed the way. The general election of 1885 convinced him that 'Ireland has now spoken; and that an effort ought to be made *by the Government* without delay to meet her demands for the management of an Irish legislative body of Irish as distinct from Imperial affairs' (Matthew, 1990, pp. 451, 455).

Gladstone bided his time, for he still hoped that the Conservative administration of Lord Salisbury would tackle the problem, a hope by no means ill-founded if their flirtation with Parnell was anything to go by. But the Conservatives drew the line at any such radical constitutional solution that might threaten to dismember the United Kingdom. Gladstone's hand was forced when on 17 December 1885 his son Herbert disclosed his thinking. But he still held the initiative. By keeping his thoughts to himself throughout the election period, by refusing to be drawn by Parnell, he was in a position to oblige Parnell to co-operate on his, Gladstone's, terms.

Parnell and the home-rule party had expected, at best, a reform of local government. Gladstone's concept of home rule was as much a surprise to them as to anyone else, even though he had asked for, and in November finally received, Parnell's own sketch of parliamentary self-government for Ireland. Whatever Gladstone had on offer, however, was what the home rulers must accept. They were in no position to sit in isolation or to renegotiate Gladstonian home rule. Gladstone's bill proposed to establish a legislature in Ireland, with an executive responsible to it. Westminster would retain control of all matters affecting the Crown, defence, foreign affairs, customs and excise; and the tax-raising powers of the Irish government would be narrowly circumscribed. Irish representation in Westminster would cease (though Gladstone agreed to reconsider this potentially separatist item). Home rule was to Gladstone the only means of bringing Ireland to social as well as political stability. He was prepared to leave the work of making proprietors out of tenants to a new Irish Parliament, but his desire to appease Earl Spencer, whom he regarded (with John Morley) as key figures in the winning of the bulk of his party to home rule, obliged him to offer a land-purchase measure as part of his settlement plan. This was only a means to the greater end, and the land-purchase part of his policy was dropped, once 'fermentation' had begun to work well on his colleagues (Jenkins, 1988, p. 278).

Gladstone saw his proposed legislation as a means of reconciling Ireland and Great Britain, but it encountered a storm of protest, not only from British Conservatives and Irish Protestants, but even from a section of his own Liberal party. In retrospect this panic is hard to understand; Gladstone went out of his way to stress that the sovereignty of the Westminster Parliament was not in jeopardy. But his critics based their opposition on several serious grounds, which could not lightly be set aside. The bill might be unworkable, for the question of Irish representation at Westminster was a vexed one. To leave them out not only looked separatist, it also deprived Ireland of a legitimate voice in matters which affected her interests. But to put them in was to give Ireland a parliament of her own and a voice in Westminster, which no other British national group enjoyed. Then there was the question of how the Irish government would treat its Protestant minority, and here the question of Irish nationalism itself came into focus: was the history of Parnellism one that would justify Gladstone's assertion that the bill would be a final settlement of the Anglo-Irish account? Was not Irish nationalism based on a hatred of Britain and a dislike of the 'Protestant Garrison' in Ireland? Had not Irish nationalism been associated with law-breaking and moonlighting in the Land League era? Had not home rulers talked of invading Ulster? Were there not darker undercurrents, calling for revenge for the degradation of the seventeenth and eighteenth centuries? And, above all, could England afford to let her United Kingdom, which she had constructed over the centuries, break up, at the very time when other European nations like Germany and Italy were consolidating their territory and power? Home rule was, then, a crisis for Ireland, the United Kingdom and the whole future of the British people; it must be resisted.

Within Ireland the question assumed an even more acute form. Parliament might debate and decide, but the Irish Protestants were unlikely to watch its stately proceedings with calm and easy minds. Irish Protestants were by no means a homogeneous group. Presbyterian Dissenters and Church of Ireland ministers had old rivalries, and a history of edgy suspicion of each others' religion and politics. Presbyterian tenant farmers were often at odds with their Anglican landlords; Protestant working men had different interests from their employers; urban Protestants had little in common with rural farmers. From 1867 Liberals – mainly Presbyterians supported by Presbyterian and Roman Catholic voters – contested and won seats in Ulster. Then there were the distinctions between northern and southern Protestants. Southern Protestants were few in number, mainly (though not exclusively) middle-class and led by landlords. Northern Protestants represented the whole spectrum of society and were populist in politics and more inclined to evangelicalism in religion. It would be wrong to brand northern Protestantism as essentially sectarian and southern Protestantism as more liberal, for the binding link was the political culture that their religion created and sustained, and a common Protestantism could and did surface before 1886. But the northern Protestants could at least hope to organize themselves as a distinct and durable political force, one that could stand up and be counted if matters came to a crisis. But all Irish Protestants counted themselves lucky that in 1886 the British Parliament voted against Gladstonian home rule for they were taken by surprise. They had little organizational preparation, and Protestant voted against Protestant in the general election of November–December 1885 and even in the home-rule election of July 1886 (Buckland, 1973, pp. 5–7, 13–14).

Irish Protestants had many grounds for opposing home rule. In the north they could point to the prosperity that their industries, especially shipbuilding, brought to the city of Belfast, a city which had long ago surpassed Dublin as the commercial capital of Ireland. They argued that an Irish Parliament, dominated by rural-based nationalists, would drain Ulster's prosperity and discriminate against her industries. They drew upon, and helped refresh, communal memories of past conflicts, when the Catholic majority had threatened their lives and liberty. Irish Protestants, including northern ones, were of course capable of living with Roman Catholics in reasonable amity if the constitution were not in question. Thus disestablishment was resented, but caused no great stir amongst the Protestant masses, and land reform was welcome to tenant farmers. Popular Protestant political leaders, such as William Johnston of Ballykilbeg, who challenged the political establishment, were wont to emerge. Protestants in the 1870s had shown a lively interest in pursuing their social and economic goals, voting for Liberals or independent candidates. But home rule was different: this would mean a major and irreversible shift of power within Ireland. Protestantism would become politically impotent; Protestant liberties would be crushed; the Protestant faith would die out, destroyed by the power of Rome. In an era of popular, if not mass democratic politics, it was unlikely that Ulster Protestants, in particular, would submit to such a fate. Gladstone was right in 1885 when he identified the Irish democracy, as it was then constituted, as having spoken clearly and unequivocally for home rule; but he ignored the claims of another democracy, now on the march, which would resist those claims to the uttermost.

The home rule crisis was fought within the British political parties, on the hustings, in Parliament and in the country. It provoked a new and significant alignment in British politics, when the Liberal party split, losing a radical group led by Joseph Chamberlain and a Whig group led by the Marquis of Hartington. The Liberal Unionists, as they called themselves, remained independent, but naturally drifted ever closer to the Conservatives. The Conservatives now began to call themselves Unionists, and the Irish Unionists were part and parcel of that British Unionist party, but one that kept a wary eye on the senior English partners of the Unionist alliance. The Irish home rulers became firmly attached to an alliance with the Liberals. This circumscribed their freedom of action and provoked stresses within the home-rule party in the future, but on balance the advantage lay with the home rulers, who found that the image of Liberalism elevated them from dangerous separatists (and possibly men of violence) to a new status as part of Liberal Britain. Nationalism benefitted from this positive image and was regarded as more progressive than it really was. In contrast,

Irish Unionism's association with British Conservatism branded it as reactionary, anti-progressive, and therefore an obstacle to reasonable politics and political solutions.

In June 1886 Gladstone, in one of the greatest and most moving performances of his career, laid his Home Rule Bill before the House of Commons. He urged the house to think not only of now, but of years to come, and it is tempting to see Gladstonian home rule as the Irish settlement that might have been. But the weaknesses in the plan, the Unionist opposition, and the doubtful nature of the whole enterprise must make for a cautious assessment of the notion that here indeed was, or could have been, a final solution of the Irish question. In any event the Home Rule Bill was defeated on 8 June 1886 by 343 votes to 313, with 93 Liberals voting against. In elections the following July the British and Irish Unionists won 316 seats, 78 anti-home-rule Liberals (Liberal Unionists) were returned, 191 Gladstonian Liberals and 85 home rulers. In Ulster the results carried little comfort for Unionists: here the Unionists won fifteen seats, Liberal Unionists two and nationalists sixteen. This result explains the perpetual anxiety of Unionists in Ulster as long as home rule was a live issue: they had an enemy within – the northern Roman Catholic.

The defeat of home rule ushered in a Unionist government. It also created difficulties for Parnell and the newly created Liberal alliance. Parnell was anxious to keep the home rule question on the British political stage. He made only infrequent visits to Ireland, partly for reasons of his liaison with Mrs Katharine O'Shea, the wife of one of his MPs, Captain William O'Shea, and he had no wish to go back to the rousing but dangerous days of his rise to power. But some of his followers wanted to retain closer links with the roots of Irish nationalism, and especially the land question. In 1887 John Dillon and William O'Brien organized the 'Plan of Campaign', by which tenants on selected estates were encouraged to offer a 'fair rent' to landlords and to withhold all payment of rent until this was accepted. Parnell was embarrassed by this direct action and distanced himself from the plan, though he took no steps to suppress it, explaining later that he was ill at the time and that the plan would, in his belief 'in the natural course' have been 'gradually succeeded by a method of agrarian organisation which I have for some time been engaged in maturing and which would have been . . . free from those defects, those political defects, which were incidental to the Plan of Campaign and which would have absolutely corresponded in every respect with the system of organisation known as trades unionism in this country' (Geary, 1986, p. 89).

The Unionist government took appropriate measures to counteract the campaign, but it was, after all, a British government. It could not be seen to be offering mere repression as the whole of its Irish policy. In 1887 the government extended the benefits of the 1881 Land act to leaseholders, and provided for the revision of all 'judicial rents' (rents fixed by land courts) affected by the decline in agricultural prices since 1881. Salisbury described this act as a necessity to win Liberal Unionist support, and to appease the left wing of his own party (Jackson, 1989, p. 133). In 1891 the government advanced land legislation a stage further. After much consultation with the landlord interest, and significant amendments, A. J. Balfour, the Irish chief secretary, steered a land bill through the commons which provided an extra thirty-three million pounds for the purchase of estates. The money, however, was to be supplied to the tenant not in cash but in government stock. Balfour had considered compulsory purchase, only to reject this after consultation with the landlords, but it was clear that if the preservation of the Union required putting pressure – limited pressure – on Irish landlords, then that option was acceptable to a Unionist government.

Parnell's embarrassment over the plan of campaign was real, but his hand was strengthened by his persistent argument that only a Liberal government could deliver home rule and that the tide would flow in his direction again. He was thus able to use British politics to influence Irish politics, but this was perhaps a sign of his neglect of his constituency, and the danger of British politics not working in his favour was real. However, after 1888, Parnell could point to a 'flowing tide'. He was helped by efforts of *The Times* to associate him with the Phoenix

Park murders of 1882, through a forgery committed by Richard Pigott, a journalist who had been in nationalist politics but had now fallen on hard times. When in 1889 the forgery was exposed, Parnell found himself vindicated in the eyes of the law and popular with British public opinion, always ready to rally to the victim of unjust accusation. The Liberal party, the vehicle of his strategy, now began to win by-elections; and the Unionist government watched its majority shrink from 188 in 1886 to 70 by 1890. There were still many obstacles in the way of home rule: Irish Unionist opposition and the Unionist-dominated house of lords. But Parnell was looking increasingly like what he wanted by now to be: an imperial statesman, ranking with Gladstone as the saviour of Ireland and Great Britain, and upholding the whole philosophy of responsible government freely given and freely accepted.

All this was jeopardized and then destroyed by Captain O'Shea's citation of Parnell as co-respondent in his divorce case against his wife, a case which he won, with no defence from Parnell, on 17 November 1890. Parnell initially secured the support of the Irish parliamentary party, but when Gladstone consulted his Liberal colleagues he realized that he could not deliver home rule if Parnell remained leader of the Irish party. On 25 November the party, at a meeting in Westminster, re-elected Parnell as its chairman for the coming session. But it did so without knowledge of Gladstone's position and attitude. When his views were disclosed, on 26 November, the party was obliged to choose between its great leader and its political goal. A meeting on 1 December in committee room 15 turned out to be a bitter and acrimonious debate, in which Parnell sought to postpone a vote on his leadership. But on 6 December Justin McCarthy, vice-chairman of the party, called on those who thought Parnell should stand down to leave and follow him: forty-three left; twenty-seven, and Parnell, remained behind.

Parnell now fought to stay what he had been for so long – the chief. But he had already made his own position more, not less, difficult by publishing a manifesto to the Irish people on 29 November, denouncing the very political connection that had been the cornerstone of the party's policy: the Liberal alliance. This made the choice more stark, and Parnell's leadership a possible liability to the parliamentary party. Moreover, the Roman Catholic Church, which Parnell had, necessarily, cultivated for its influence in Irish politics, was unlikely to throw its weight behind an adulterer. And even the lower clergy, whose views had deviated from the bishops' line on political issues in the past, were less attached to Parnell since his neglect of local Irish politics, and especially the plan of campaign. Even before he began his fight back Parnell had a number of important fences to mend, yet his formidable powers, the appeal of his great name, his support in urban areas, where he now championed the needs and rights of the working man, and his attraction for the young, all gave him a power to wound his enemies, if not to destroy them.

Such a campaign, fought in such circumstances, could only harm the cause of parliamentarianism in Ireland, but Parnell was careful not to attach himself too closely to the more radical nationalist forces that rallied to his call. His fundamental argument was that he, and he alone, could stand in Westminster and prise self-government out of Gladstone and the Liberals. He would not go beyond constitutional means, but he appreciated the views of those who would go beyond these means, should he fail. It was a measure of his desperation that Parnell even went to Ulster, there to warn his followers of the need to reconcile, and not seek merely to overpower, Ulster Unionist opposition to home rule (Bew, 1980, pp. 128–9).

Parnell's last campaign ended with his death on 6 October 1891. His struggle was a hopeless one, lacking a solid base among the traditional elements that made up the bedrock of Irish nationalist politics: the Church, the farmers, the middle classes. The tragedy of Parnell was to haunt many generations of Irishmen, and his titanic struggle was to be held up as a shame to the Irish people, who had deserted their leader in his hour of need. But in a sense nothing much was altered by Parnell's tragedy. The Church and nationalist politics were still combined; the Irish party that had abandoned Parnell retained the policies of its lost leader; and Gladstone was still committed to delivering home rule for Ireland. In the general election of

July 1892 nine Parnellites were returned as against seventy-one anti-Parnellites. Gladstone's election victory in Britain placed home rule once more before the House of Commons. In 1893 Gladstone introduced his second Home Rule Bill. Once again Unionist Ulster girded its loins to defend itself, and there was now talk of the need to resist by armed force if need be. An Ulster Defence Union was founded, but the Unionists' failure to put up any sign of serious or well-organized resistance was to lull nationalists and Liberals into a false sense of security (Buckland, 1973, p. 17). In the event, no such defence was needed, for whereas the bill was approved by the Commons, it was defeated in the Lords. Gladstone did not take his campaign to the country. He resigned, and left the Liberal party with the doubtful legacy of the party that stood for Irish home rule, almost to the neglect of other (British) interests.

Nationalism and Unionism emerged from the home-rule era as the dominant political ideologies of modern Ireland. Yet their apparent homogeneity must not disguise the fact that they were based upon societies in the process of change. Rural Ireland was no longer able to hold the stage of politics alone. Urban voices, especially among working-class leaders in Dublin and Belfast, were soon to be heard. Landlords were not the force they had been in 1890. Presbyterians no longer provided a solid base of Liberal support. Ulster Catholics no longer supported Liberals, but now looked to nationalist politics to achieve their goals. They were soon to have a voice hitherto denied them in the home-rule party. But there remained an underlying sectarianism in Irish life which, while it must not be exaggerated, shaped the lives and perceptions of the vast bulk of her people. The increasingly popular character of Irish politics played upon, but did not fundamentally change, this central division. Indeed, in many respects it exacerbated it.

5

Makers of a new Ireland, 1891–1910

Ireland's experience under the Union resulted in two parallel, and perhaps related, developments. Since Britain was the governing power, and since Ireland sent representatives to Westminster who might hope to influence government, but could not aspire to form an administration, Irish electors never experienced the full measure of control involved in choosing a government directly responsive to their wishes. It was therefore necessary to wait upon England's pleasure and to hope, as O'Connell and Parnell had hoped, for political conditions at Westminster to turn to their advantage. Irish Protestants experienced the same predicament, and they too had to search for a niche in a British political party, with, as it happened, a reasonable degree of success. But after the Parnell disaster it was held, at least among an elite, that the trouble with Ireland was precisely her determination to wait upon events in Great Britain, and to neglect the possibility of achieving change or improvement for herself. Moreover, the disarray in which the Nationalists found themselves after 1891, and the failure of the whole home rule strategy, meant that Ireland was given a breathing-space after the crises of home rule and Unionism. This might, some believed, turn out to her benefit.

The second development was the surge of writing about Ireland, Irish writers reflecting upon their predicament. This was not as arcane as it seemed. The role of an intelligentsia can be exaggerated, yet the image of a country, the way in which it presents itself to the world (which in Irish terms always meant England) can help shape the self-perception of even the least literary of people. It can also shape the popular perception of political leaders and present them in heroic and epic form (or diminish them and denigrate their memory). But the special predicament of Ireland caused writers to follow two main trends. They often set out to explain to the average Englishman that Ireland was not the peculiar and backward place he believed it to be (as William Carlton and Charles James Kickham did) or they found themselves locked into the nationalist mode, with their patriotism called in question if they dared do other than praise their country (as Thomas Davis praised it).

It might reasonably be held, therefore, that Irishmen needed liberation from the tendency to wait upon Englishmen to act on their behalf, and that Irish writers needed to be freed from the demands of politics, especially nationalist politics. These ideas were connected by the conviction, increasingly held, that it was up to Ireland to do something for herself: an idea given force by the spectacle of Parnell clinging to the Liberal alliance between 1886 and 1889, and then finding that it was, seemingly, incompatible with what he defined in his last campaign as the true interests of Ireland. This political event had cultural repercussions, since it was taken by many to signify what was wrong in the whole dependency culture that Ireland had, all unwittingly, adopted since the Act of Union.

Ireland could do it for herself: she could create her own cultural, social and economic regeneration. And this had an added advantage: if Ireland could create a new sense of pride, of self-respect, even define herself anew, then the vexed political divisions occasioned by the crisis of home rule would disappear. A united Ireland could transform herself easily, painlessly, into a free Ireland, a land free in all senses of the word: an Ireland enjoying something richer and more enduring than mere devolutionary government.

But it was not only the Irish who sought to establish a firm grip on what they regarded as their benighted country. Paradoxically, the impetus for change came from the British government, indeed from a Conservative government, intent upon making the Union a reality. If Irish nationalism was – as A. J. Balfour believed – the result of material grievances, then the removal of these grievances would reveal the hollowness within. The Scots were a more genuinely national people, yet the Scots had settled down to live happily under the Union. This would be possible because England held the money needed for a renewal and reform of Irish life; she could undertake what Ireland could not do for herself. The question, however, was not whether she had the money, but, rather, if her political will was sufficient to enable her to attend to the wants of what was after all a peripheral region. There was inevitably a mood of impatience with the grievance-chasing politicians of Ireland – all of them – which Balfour expressed when in 1896 he complained that 'all the Irish members will invariably come down to the House and press for money when they think it can be squeezed out of the treasury' (quoted by Boyce, in Brady, 1989, p. 150).

And so there was ambivalence, even as the Unionists set their faces towards reform and good government in Ireland. Still, reforms did come, even if they had to be reconciled to the exigencies of the parliamentary timetable and take their chance along with other, more pressing demands of government. Local government reform in 1898 placed the bulk of local institutions in popular, and therefore nationalist hands. State aid for the less prosperous parts of the country (the 'congested districts' where the rateable value was less than thirty shillings per head of the population) was administered by a Congested Districts Board, established in 1891, which oversaw the building of harbours, the encouragement of local industries (such as fishing) and the improvement of agricultural measures. The Unionists returned to the land question, which both parties had by now identified as one that lay at the root of Irish discontent, but which the Unionists in particular made their own concern, since it would undermine the demand for home rule. Parnell had favoured the policy of land purchase, of settling the tenants on the land and developing a peasant proprietory. Michael Davitt opposed this as simply another form of private ownership and the creation of a new set of small-scale landlords. In one sense, this dispute was becoming irrelevant by the 1890s, when the real enemy of Irish rural prosperity was neither the landlord nor the tenant, but backward agricultural methods and competition from foreign produce: grain, meat and butter. Nor would peasant proprietorship end the reign of the graziers, who turned land over to pasture and thus jeopardized rural employment. It would not help those smaller and middling farmers to whom cattle rearing provided only a moderate, or even an inadequate living. But land purchase was politically attractive: it would appease nationalists and would end the conflict between landlord and tenant.

The problem was that, so far, the Unionists' efforts to encourage and support land purchase seemed only to aggravate the problem. Balfour's 1891 Land Act proved unpopular with landlord and tenant alike, because of its complicated financial arrangements and its use of government stock instead of cash as payment for purchase. Landlords were not anxious to give up the political game, but they knew where their economic interests lay and they were no longer a force in local government. Any influence they still possessed did not depend upon their ability to bring pressure to bear on their tenants. The Land League had indeed weakened, if not broken, the grip of the landlords, and their economic plight had few sympathizers on the other side of the Irish Sea. They were ready for a resolution of the problem, and so were the tenants. But the important point of the settlement that emerged was that it saw one of the rare occasions when Irish people of different persuasions co-operated in a joint enterprise, one over which the British government presided, but did not initiate or direct it.

In December 1902 a conference representing landlords and tenants met, under Lord Dunraven, a landlord from County Limerick and a man of liberal disposition. When they reached agreement the Irish chief secretary, George Wyndham, used their deliberations as the basis for a new Land Act. There were other reasons why government response was necessary. In 1902 there were stirrings in Ulster, where an independent candidate inspired by T. W. Russell (a Protestant and Unionist, but a radical in land reform) stood for and won East Down. Another independent victory followed in North Fermanagh in 1903. Ulster tenant farmers were as anxious as anyone else to push the landlords in the direction of land purchase. It was clearly in the Unionist interest to take a firm grip on the issue, and in 1903 a Land Act offered generous compensation to landlords and good rates of interest to the purchasing tenants. This Act required amendment, and in 1909 the Liberal government was obliged to amend it, giving the Congested Districts Board powers of compulsory purchase, and increasing the finance available for tenant purchase, but it proved the decisive breakthrough in moves – until then uncertain and halting – towards making a tenant proprietory the core of Irish rural society.

The fact that Irishmen had co-operated was significant; the fact that British government had moved but slowly before then was equally important. It was a symptom, or so some held, of the problem of making the Union work for Ireland; delays, politics, prejudice, stood in the way of speedy remedy. Sir Horace Plunkett, a Unionist landlord with an interest in modern agricultural methods, also found that it was imperative for progressive Irishmen to encourage even a Unionist government. In 1889 he launched a co-operative movement, and by 1894 he had succeeded in creating an Irish Agricultural Organization Society. He continued to press for government action, and in 1898 a Department of Agriculture and Technical Instruction for Ireland was established, with Plunkett in charge. He was keenly interested in the failure of his country to move with the times, which he attributed to 'certain defects of character, not ethically grave, but economically paralysing': lack of moral courage, initiative, independence and self-reliance. For this reason he admired all movements in Ireland which aspired to build up Irish self-reliance, and thus 'exert a stimulating influence upon our moral life' (Plunkett, 1909, p. viii).

Plunkett believed that the new spirit, embodied in the 1902 Dunraven initiative, was not – as English observers believed – because Irishmen had suddenly 'put away childish things and learned to behave like grown-up Englishmen'. Rather it was because of the new 'philosophy of Irish progress', the acknowledgement by Irishmen of their responsibility for themselves. Plunkett did not blame England for Ireland's tardy development; rather he pointed the finger at the Roman Catholic Church for its resistance to modernization; whereas, in contrast, the north of Ireland displayed 'thrift, industry, and enterprise' which he associated with the Presbyterian community there. Plunkett was not blind to the sectarianism of the north, where employers accepted or rejected workers on grounds of religion. Nevertheless, the lack of enterprise in the Catholic south was, he believed, due to a 'defect in the industrial character of Roman Catholics' and the influence of their authoritarian religion. Thus Plunkett, Southern Irish Unionist though he was, was anxious to keep Ulster in the nation and to ensure that it played its full part in the making of a new Ireland (Ibid., pp. 8, 90, 100–2).

Plunkett's efforts were not confined to the industrial and agricultural spheres. His magazine, the *Irish Homestead*, was edited by George Russell (AE), a northerner by birth but a leading literary figure in the Dublin of his day. The *Homestead* published work by young Irish writers, and it sought once again to give Irishmen an opportunity to display their talents before an Irish audience, instead of making the pilgrimage to the literary world of the metropolis. This was symptomatic of the new mood that followed the fall of Parnell. Irish writers had indeed sought to create a literary revival before 1891. Thomas Davis had founded a tradition of literary nationalism. Sir Samuel Ferguson, another northerner and Unionist who came to develop a love of Irish literature, attempted in the 1860s to direct public attention away from the divisive world of politics to cultural pursuits that might bring them together in a common appreciation of the Irish past (necessarily a distant past, since the recent past was anything but common). In 1878 Standish O'Grady embarked on the publication of his histories of the heroic Irish age, an age of Gods and Celtic chieftains, who seemed to stand for all that was heroic and mystical in the Irish mind. This had the advantage of portraying the Irish, not as a Catholic people or a Christian people at all, but as a naturally pagan race. Shorn of sectarianism, deprived of religion, the

67

Irish became a race to which non-Catholics like himself could happily belong (Cairns and Richards, 1988, pp. 51–7).

It is no coincidence that this kind of writing, which inspired the great literary revival of the 1890s, first made its appearance in the 1870s, for the 1870s were an age of Tory democracy and of much speculation about what democracy would mean for Britain and Ireland. This democracy was limited when compared to the mass democracy of the twentieth century, but it was not so regarded at the time. The fear of the masses – widely felt in England – was given a special sharpness in Ireland by the fact that these would be Catholic masses. And it is no surprise therefore that the inspiration behind the revival should come from those who were not from the masses, but from a Protestant ascendancy background. To say this is not to imply that they were from landed backgrounds; W. B. Yeats, the revival's most famous exemplar, was of firmly middle-class stock. But, like O'Grady, he identified with an aristocracy, and sought to identify the Irish aristocracy with the Irish peasantry. Together they would make a stand against materialism and philistinism, a stand for the Protestant people, who had contributed so much to Ireland and who were now threatened with extinction by the middle class and the urban mob.

The fall of Parnell released Irish writing from political shackles, or so Yeats, Lady Gregory, AE, George Moore and Edward Martyn, the leading figures of the revival, believed. Yet they found that they must hunt with the nationalist hounds if they were to run with the non-nationalist hares. Yeats flung himself into nationalist politics of the most radical kind, participating in the efforts of the more 'advanced' men to commemorate the centenary of the 1798 rebellion, and protesting against the proposed visit by King Edward VII to Ireland in 1903. He wrote one of the most influential of the 'self-sacrifice for Ireland' plays ever performed on the Irish stage, *Cathleen ni Houlihan*. But his purpose in founding the National Literary Society in 1892 (in London) was to create an Irish literature in the English language which would place Ireland in the forefront of the nations of Europe, and give her a reputation for great writing, instead of easy buffoonery.

Nationalists welcomed any initiative that seemed to imply that Ireland was as great, or greater, than England, that she was no inferior nation. But they failed to follow Yeats in his pursuit of the excellent. They found fault with the kind of material that he wanted to publish, and Yeats suffered a defeat when Charles Gavan Duffy, the former Young Irelander, took over the new 'Library of Ireland' and turned its publications into Davisite literature: books that lacked critical style and simply reinforced the stereotypes beloved of Irish nationalism. The essential difference between the revivalists and nationalists was publicly revealed when the plays of the Literary Theatre, founded in Dublin in 1901, met with a hostile reception from their Irish audience. In particular, J. M. Synge's *Playboy of the Western World*, produced in 1907, with its vigorous portrayal of peasant life and its earthy language, was denounced as a slur upon the Irish nation.

It was, however, much deeper than this. It was a celebration of an energetic, grotesque, but living individualism in the face of twentieth-century anonymity. It challenged the orthodoxy, the conformity, the puritanism of Irish Catholic life. But the play, and Catholic reaction to it, revealed how hard it was for the Protestant Irish to offer leadership and what they regarded as enlightenment to their Catholic fellow-countrymen. It was difficult for them to appreciate the sensitivity of Catholics to their social origins, and to Protestant interpretations of Irish life. This problem had of course dogged Sir Horace Plunkett as well. Yet the question of a Protestant role in a Catholic Ireland might be approached from another angle, this time through the revival of the Irish language, and the remoulding of Ireland in the image of her lost Gaelic past.

It is not surprising that the search for cultural origins should find a place in Irish politics, as it did in the politics of other dependent European countries. In 1884 Michael Cusack founded the Gaelic Athletic Association, with the Roman Catholic Archbishop Croke of Cashel as its patron. The association's purpose was to replace foreign (English) games with native Irish sports such as hurling, and to replace also any foreigners whose unwanted presence would be discovered by their desire to play the foreign games of soccer, rugby, or cricket. Policemen and members of the armed forces were excluded from the GAA. But the cultural revival of the 1890s was of a rather different stamp. The man most closely associated with the Gaelic revival was Douglas Hyde, of Protestant and (like Yeats) of middle-class background. Hyde had only contempt for those among the Catholic masses who, since O'Connell's time were, as he put it in a wounding line 'crawling to social position'. But he also criticized the Protestant for his lack of national concern, for ignoring the wrongs inflicted upon his nation. In 1893 the Gaelic League was founded, with Hyde, Eoin MacNeill (a Catholic Ulsterman) and Fr Eugene O'Growney at its head. Hyde hoped to define an Irish 'race', but one that would give his people a place, since they could identify with an ancient Irish lineage, an Irish aristocracy, a heroic period of Irish past, to which the Irish Protestant ascendancy could gain entry. Ireland moulded the race, and everyone was included, unless – like the stubborn 'Saxons' of the north – they refused to embrace their mother, Ireland. Once again Ireland could be shorn of her Catholic character. But this was a short-lived triumph. D. P. Moran, an influential, clever, but acerbic writer, denounced the idea that the 'Anglo-Irish' were in fact 'Irish'. The Gaelic and Catholic identities were fused; Anglo-Ireland was British Ireland, Protestant Ireland and Unionist Ireland. Moran's vigilant eye also detected the essentially anti-modernist outlook of Hyde and his like. He denounced their love of the peasant, looking to a Gaelic, Catholic, urban middle class as the means of taking Ireland into the new century with her head held high. This was an exciting concept, for it sought to combine the modern with the Gaelic tradition, seeking to realize a vision of a new nation based upon a historical language and culture (Cairns and Richards, 1988, pp. 91–2).

The fusion of traditional and modern found another voice, this time a more unexpected one, in the writings of James Connolly. Connolly, born in Edinburgh of Irish parents, was a Marxist, and a believer in the progress of mankind. He accepted the need for society to be organized on scientific lines, but he saw in ancient Gaelic Ireland a primitive form of communism.

He believed that Gaelic society had been a society of equals and he held that to recreate that equal society Ireland must first throw off the shackles of British rule, since the British state was a capitalist state. He had no time for the capitalists of north-east Ulster; the Ulster Protestant was deluded and fooled by his Unionist employers. Though probably not himself a believer, he held that the Roman Catholic Church also stood for creating social equality – or at least, in its pure form, its doctrine could be so construed. In a real sense, therefore, Moran's and Connolly's visions were revolutionary, and they helped inspire the Easter Rising of 1916 (Boyce, 1991, pp. 300–4).

This exciting prospect could not gain more than a limited attention if it did not move beyond the pages of Moran's publication, the *Leader*, and Connolly's *Workers' Republic*. But Arthur Griffith, a journalist and political thinker, hoped to broaden the base of this philosophy, and also delete some of its features most objectionable to Protestants. To this end he constructed the idea that later became known as 'Sinn Fein', 'ourselves', which expressed the notion of economic, political and cultural self-sufficiency that would be the making of a new Ireland. Griffith too was ashamed of the backwardness, the degradation of Irish society, and he wanted to make Ireland economically prosperous as well as nationally proud. His ideas were a hybrid: he admired the eighteenth-century Protestant patriots, Grattan and Flood, Swift and Tone, but he wanted Ireland to be a Gaelic nation. Yet he envisaged a place for non-Irish speakers in his Ireland, and he began with a favourable disposition towards the literary revival. He wanted to construct a constitutional arrangement between Great Britain and Ireland which, like that of the late eighteenth century, retained the British sovereign as the symbol of the fact that the ocean forbade division between the two countries; but he also wanted an Irish Parliament as a recognition that the sea forbade Union. He took as his tactical model the 1867 Austro-Hungarian settlement, when Hungarian patriots withdrew from Vienna and established themselves in Budapest until the Austrians conceded their demand for autonomy. He believed that Ireland needed tariff barriers to protect her industries, yet he saw Belfast and its industrial character as essential for Irish prosperity, ignoring the fact that Belfast feared tariff barriers as an obstacle to its economic development. His Cumann na nGaedheal movement, founded in 1900, was less of a political party than a movement which would permeate Irish society and then, through an electoral mandate, prise away England's grip on Ireland, while leaving the Crown as a symbol which would satisfy Unionists and give them their place in the brotherhood of the Irish (Boyce, 1990, p. 223).

Griffith's broad appeal encountered the difficulties such appeals generally faced: suspicion from nationalists because he welcomed Unionists into the nation; suspicion from the Catholic Church because he spoke approvingly of the literary revival, that nest of Protestant values; suspicion from the Church because Griffith supported urban development and threatened the values of rural Ireland; suspicion from the electorate because withdrawal from Westminster took Irish representatives away from the very centres of power where they were at last getting some of what they wanted. A Catholic university was approved in 1908, better land legislation in 1909, old-age pensions in 1908 (which cost the Treasury £2,400,000 for Ireland within two years) (Doherty and Hickey, 1989, p. 176).

Nationalist Ireland was not dead and gone after 1891, even if it experienced a period of misfortune and division. The basic material of the movement – the Roman Catholic Church, the farmers, the aspiring political elite who might yet sit in triumph in Dublin, the publicans who cut a dash locally – all were still firmly attached to the nationalist cause, and could yet be rallied behind a nationalist party, if only that party could revitalize itself and heal the divisions that followed the Parnell split. New hope was given in the last couple of years of the nineteenth century. The Boer War gave nationalists a long-awaited opportunity to twist the British lion's tail, to identify with an oppressed people (the Afrikaaners) and to gloat over British defeats in the war. An Irish 'Transvaal Committee' was founded to mobilize support for the Boers. This coincided with the interest aroused by the centenary of the 1798 rebellion which (although it provoked disagreement between nationalists over whose legacy the '98 really was, and who should play the leading part in its celebration) none the less brought nationalists some much-needed publicity. What they now needed was a revitalized organization, and this was provided in the United Irish League, founded by the parliamentarian William O'Brien in 1898.

In January 1898 O'Brien took nationalist Ireland back to its roots, back to Westport, County Mayo, the scene of the formation of the Land League in 1879. He went back, too, to its slogan of 'the land for the people'. O'Brien was an energetic and able politician; he was also, to an unusual extent, a far-sighted one. He feared what he perceived as dangerous developments in Irish nationalism: its neglect of grass-roots support, especially in the west, which was still suffering from high emigration and poor standards of living, and its blindness to the Protestant question, especially the strong Unionism of the north. His United Irish League raised the problems faced by the smallholders of the west, and the harsh conditions imposed upon them, not so much by landlords as by graziers. O'Brien's hope was that the experience of the land war could be repeated, with the political mobilization of rural areas in the cause of land reform and nationalism. But his success, though only partial, convinced the quarrelling parliamentarians that they had better unite or lose their predominance in nationalist politics. The Catholic Church too urged unity in the interests of strength, especially the exertion of pressure at Westminster to coax educational measures out of the British government. When at last the parliamentary party negotiated its reunification on 30 January 1900, it did so under the leadership of John Redmond, but without any discernible policy, other than that which had dominated its thinking since the 1880s: to combine, to bring together those who belonged together (Catholics and nationalists) and to look to British politics to provide the means of attaining home rule.

O'Brien's concern for nationalists to establish better relations with Unionists was no more successful. In his opinion, the 1903 land conference pointed the way forward: 'Conference plus business' could be transferred from the economic to the political sphere. O'Brien was almost certainly over-optimistic; landlords might relinquish large tracts of their property, but they would not necessarily therefore relinquish their efforts to keep Ireland in the Union. Still, the defeat of home rule in 1893, and the subsequent relaxation of the high pressure of Protestant tensions in the 1890s, resulted in a slackening of Unionist determination, or so it seemed. Even in Ulster political mavericks appeared. T. M. Russell was active among the tenant farmers. Independent Orangemen manifested themselves to challenge the official movement. Protestant working men showed signs that they would combine against their (Unionist) employers. Moreover, both the British political parties seemed unwilling to match the complete commitment to Union or home rule that had characterized their behaviour in 1886 and 1893. First the Unionists, in 1904, toyed with the idea of devolution of an administrative kind to meet what was indeed a real need for Irish people to play a greater part in the government of their country. This raised a storm of protest in Irish Unionist ranks, and in December 1904 a Unionist conference in Belfast called for action to resist devolution and resolved to form an Ulster council to 'bring into line all local Unionist associations in the province of Ulster' (Buckland, 1973, pp. 19–21).

In March 1905 the result of this crisis was seen: the first meeting of the Ulster Unionist Council in Belfast, followed by the resignation of the Irish secretary, George Wyndham, driven from office as a result of Unionist pressure. The formation of the Ulster Unionist Council was one of the most significant events in the political history of modern Ireland. The Council was composed of 200 representatives, a hundred nominated by local Unionist associations, fifty by the Orange Order, and the remaining fifty divided among MPs, peers and ex-officio members. Its importance lay in its focusing of Irish Unionism in the Ulster region, thus, for the first time, providing Ulster Unionism with a local identity. Hitherto, the sense of its Ulster roots was regarded as in no significant way compromising it connections with Unionists of the rest of Ireland, and even its sense of Irishness. But it also marked another departure from nineteenth-century Unionism. Now the centre of the organization was Belfast, and Belfast offered all the advantages of modern politics: easy mobilization of Unionists; access to modern publicity methods; access to the British newspaper press and to the European press. Rural unionism could not of course be ignored; landlords still counted for something in the Unionist hierarchy. But the driving force behind modern Unionism lay in its industrial heartland; and this in turn enhanced its propaganda image as a progressive force in modern Ireland, contrasting with the backward rural society on which nationalist Ireland rested.

The Unionist experiment with devolution ended in the destruction of the Irish chief secretary as well as his scheme. John Redmond had initially favoured the Unionist initiative (from the safe distance of America) but his lieutenants in the Irish Parliamentary Party were less helpful, and John Dillon, in particular, attacked it as a delusion, a destroyer, not a facilitator, of home rule. Redmond now found it politic to denounce those Irish Unionists, Sir Horace Plunkett and Lord Dunraven, who through the Irish Reform Association had helped advance the Wyndham plan, and to demonstrate that, in effect, the Ulster and Irish Unionists who savaged the scheme were fully justified in their fears: 'I regard the action of these men as the greatest vindication yet of the inevitable and onward tendency of the Irish National movement,' he told nationalists in October 1905 (Bew, 1987, p. 119).

This was balm to Unionist hurt. They could close ranks and justify their behaviour, which had by no means met with approval in the Unionist cabinet, where A. J. Balfour found their hounding of Wyndham offensive. But soon it was the Liberals' turn to discover that their Irish alliance was less than easy. After the Liberal landslide in the general election of January 1906 Sir Henry Campbell-Bannerman's government had no particular need of Irish nationalist support. Nevertheless, the government embarked on a series of important reforms, establishing a Roman Catholic university system at last, amending the 1903 Land Act, introducing old-age pensions throughout the United Kingdom, providing extra finance for labourers' cottages, and enacting legislation to facilitate the construction of working-class houses. It also decided to experiment with devolution in the form of an Irish Councils Bill, which would have set up a council consisting of eighty-two elected and twenty-four nominated members plus the under-secretary for Ireland. This council would be given responsibility for a range of functions, including education boards, the Local Government Board, the Congested Districts Board and the Department of Agriculture and Technical Instruction. Once again Redmond was favourable to devolution but he was obliged to retreat and bow to the public clamour that devolution was a ploy to delay home rule, falling far short of the 'national demand'. An Irish Convention met to discuss the bill and duly rejected it, with Redmond describing the council as 'utterly inadequate in its scope' (Bew, 1987, pp. 130–3).

It was at this point that the ideas of a new Ireland, aired since the fall of Parnell, had their last chance of achieving some measure of success. William O'Brien, alarmed at the polarization of Irish politics, sought to take matters in hand, as he had done in 1898 when he founded the United Irish League, but his task was formidable. The revival and organization of Ulster Unionism was a symptom of the new role that popular politics would play in Ireland, but another sign was the emergence of Ulster Roman Catholics as a political force. The Irish Parliamentary Party had, until now, found its chief strength in the south and west; it had beaten off the challenge of Sinn Fein, defeating its opponents in the North Leitrim by-election in February 1908 by 3,103 votes to 1,157. But it found itself relying more heavily on the accession of strength that its vigorous Ulster political boss, Joseph Devlin, gave it in his Ancient Order of Hibernians movement, which was part friendly society and part vote-delivering machine. This gave the party local strength where it had lacked local organization, but it also introduced the sectarian politics of Ulster into a party always susceptible to sectarian pressures in its own right. Devlin was no bigot but a personable and tolerant man, with a real sympathy for working-class people, whatever their background. But he was essentially a representative of his Catholic people and no one else. In 1909 a Nationalist Convention met to consider the new Liberal land bill. William O'Brien found himself on the receiving end of AOH displeasure and he broke with the Parliamentary Party to form an 'All for Ireland League', based on his native Cork.

O'Brien's task was rendered almost impossible by the conflict in Westminster between Unionists and Liberals over the 1909 'People's Budget' and the veto of the House of Lords. This struggle had originally nothing to do with Ireland, but arose out of Liberal frustration with the Lords' tactical rejection or amendment of much of their ordinary legislation. In 1909 the Liberals drew up their budget, which included a tax on the value of undeveloped land. The Lords rejected it, and were accused by the government of unconstitutional behaviour. The Liberals resolved to end the veto of the Lords, which in turn had vital implications for the Irish Union, since the Lords provided a bulwark against a home-rule bill, as they had done in 1893. These implications became clear when in January 1910 a general election fought on the Lords issue resulted in the return of 275 Liberals, 273 Unionists, 40 Labour members and 70 Redmondites. A second election held in December only confirmed the state of the parties. Redmond was not the 'dictator of Westminster' that Unionist propaganda claimed. The Liberals knew that their government was one that Redmond could hardly afford to turn out, and they knew also that they could rely on the support of Labour. But Redmond was able to insist that the Liberals would fulfil their long-standing pledge on home rule in return for his support – support which was not without difficulty, for the 'People's Budget' contained clauses inimical to the interests of Irish publicans and brewers, who were a force in the nationalist movement. William O'Brien found his 'All for Ireland' support vanish in 1910 as Redmond appeared to assume the mantle of Parnell: the man who could make the Liberal alliance work, only this time with no danger of rejection by the Lords and no possibility of a split in Liberal party ranks.

Thus the era of self-regeneration, of internal renewal, ended with a return to the political tactics of the 1880s. But this was not the 1880s. New voices were being heard in Ireland, albeit still on the margins of political life, denouncing the whole concept of home rule and calling for a radical departure. In Unionist circles, the new century saw the emergence of new, populist forces, led and organized by the Belfast middle classes, who were at the heart of the political and economic life of north-east Ulster.

The would-be makers of the new Ireland failed in their central purpose of creating a sense of all-Ireland nationality, of transcending sectarian divisions. They, or some of them, failed to check the march of bourgeois Catholic Ireland towards mastery of the nation. They failed to save Ireland for the kind of hierarchical society that they discerned in the Celtic past, and now sought to revive. Plunkett's modernization and Connelly's socialism alike were quickly transformed into the nationalist idea of history. The Protestants of the north, though sometimes individually attracted to the new ideas, remained as a group steadfastly outside their central task, that of accommodating the various Irish traditions. But – though this was far from evident in 1910 – the makers of a new Ireland had provided material for a political revolution that would sweep away all that they hoped to preserve or change.

6

Nationalism versus Unionism, 1911–1918

In August 1911, after a bitter struggle, the Parliament Act became law. Whether this is seen as a step towards democracy or, as its opponents alleged, a move towards single-chamber government, it had the most serious implications for the contending parties in Ireland. No one doubted that a Home Rule Bill would shortly be placed before the House of Commons, and nothing would now stand in its way, for the House of Lords could only delay its passage, not kill it. When in April 1912 Asquith introduced the third Home Rule Bill he was at pains to point out that it stood firmly in the Gladstonian tradition, and that the sovereignty of the Westminster Parliament was in no respect compromised or diminished. There would be an Irish Parliament consisting of a nominated senate and an elected lower house, and this Parliament was given general powers to legislate for the 'peace, order and good government of Ireland' with the exception of certain excluded subjects: matters concerning the Crown, peace or war, the armed forces, defence, treaties and foreign trade, and now (in contrast to the 1893 bill) land purchase, old-age pensions and national insurance. Certain reserved powers, and in particular the troublesome question of the police forces, might be transferred to the Irish government in the fullness of time. The Ulster Protestant minority was ignored, save for a general prohibition against the government of Ireland making discriminatory laws. The number of Irish

MPs in the British House of Commons was reduced to forty-two, a rather clumsy effort at combining the need to allow Irish representation in Parliament with the desire not to give the Irish an unfair advantage over other parts of the kingdom.

This was a modest measure of self-government, but the nationalists welcomed it as the goal of all their hopes, as a final settlement of the long-standing dispute between Great Britain and Ireland. John Redmond found the bill to his liking, for he saw himself as a potential imperial statesman, joining the ranks of the Canadians, the Australians, the New Zealanders and – the latest members of the club – the South Africans in the family of nations that formed the core of the British Empire. Redmond was a kind of imperialist nationalist, and no doubt most Irish nationalists saw their future in the empire, which, after all, Irish Catholics had helped to win in the uniform of the British army, and which had offered the Roman Catholic Church in Ireland the chance to spread its word throughout so many foreign lands. Imperialist Catholicism and imperialist nationalism went together: without the imperial context the Church would have found itself a less prestigious, and certainly much less influential body.

Yet the language of home rulers in Ireland itself was often extreme: anti-English, even separatist in tone, for after all the home rule party's great leader, Parnell, had claimed that no man had the right to set bounds to the march of a nation. Irish Unionists had no doubt that the language of nationalism as used in Ireland was nearer the truth than the moderate tones now being employed at Westminster. But in any case the root of the matter for them was not just home rule: it was the consequences that flowed from home rule, which, they held, would be the creation of a Catholic ascendancy and the extirpation of their civil and religious freedom. They may have been mistaken in this perception, though they could point to nationalist speeches as evidence for their fears; but once they made up their minds, then they were prepared to follow through the consequences of their decision, even if that meant pushing resistance to the point of civil war.

The home rule crisis provided Unionism, and especially

Ulster Unionism, with just that kind of atmosphere which could mould the Protestants of the north of Ireland into a single, compact community. Ulster Protestants could be represented to Britain and the world as a distinct group of people, progressive, orderly and loyal, whose only wish was to remain in the United Kingdom, not to be handed over to their traditional enemies and the enemies of the empire. They did not base their claim, as nationalists did, on some immemorial, historical right. They based it upon their constitutional and legal rights as subjects of the Crown, but they had a lively sense of the Protestant past, which they interpreted as one of heroic resistance to oppression and tyranny. They thus telescoped that past, giving it a unity and a coherence that it hardly possessed. They did not assert a nationalist identity. On the contrary, they held that nationalism was a sham, and could not be made the basis of politics at all. It would weaken the kingdom and the empire, and open the way to the decline of both. They based their political identity on the broad description, 'British', and although this left them vulnerable to the accusation that they had no clear idea of who they were, at least in national terms, it was a workable enough definition and one comparable with the Scots, who were also able to combine local and British identities. Moreover, in 1912 England – the predominant partner – was still a self-consciously Protestant country and the idea of a Protestant people claiming the protection of a Protestant Crown was not such an odd one. Their emphasis on the Crown had another advantage; they could remain loyal to the symbol of the state, and yet refuse to obey the government that threatened to deprive them of the heritage of the state.

When Ulster Unionists set out to frustrate home rule in 1912 they retained hopes that they could prevent its application anywhere in Ireland. These hopes were shared by Sir Edward Carson, the Irish Unionist leader who placed himself at their head in their great struggle. Carson's guiding star, as he himself put it, was the Union, and the maintainance of his country within the Union. He had made his name under A. J. Balfour as crown prosecutor in the land agitation era. By now he was a highly successful lawyer, an influential member of the British

Unionist, as well as Irish Unionist, parties, and the leading representative of the Unionism that held that Ireland separate from Britain would sink into economic and political ruin. Yet he was prepared to place himself at the head of the Ulster Unionist resistance to home rule, even if that meant – as it inevitably would – making a threat of armed resistance. Carson hoped and believed that the threat would not become a reality; he had no desire to lead mob violence, sectarian riots, or even military resistance to British soldiers. But he was convinced that if the Ulster Unionists' resistance went beyond parliamentary methods, if the Ulstermen showed that they meant business, then the Liberal government would drop the Home Rule Bill, and all Ireland would be saved for the Union. The idea of an 'Ulster Covenant' was his: a signed, sober declaration to resist home rule by all means necessary, which gave an impressive demonstration of Ulster Unionist solidarity, determination and discipline, pledging the Ulster Unionists to resist home rule for the whole of Ireland.

Carson believed the Liberal government was bluffing when it threatened to impose home rule on Ireland against the resistance of the Ulster Unionists. Unfortunately, Redmond and the Liberals started from the same point: that Ulster Unionists were bluffing when they asserted their determination to defeat home rule, if need be by arms. But as the crisis deepened, a new possibility emerged: Ulster might be given some special treatment – perhaps the choice of temporarily opting out of the operation of home rule – and thus the rest of Ireland could be given what it clearly and democratically desired. But this raised other dilemmas. Redmond and the home-rule party held that Ireland was a seamless garment that could not be rent by any recognition of the claims of any special group. There were no special Irishmen, only Irishmen (though some might be more Irish than others). Yet he knew that he would find it difficult to resist a demand by the Liberals for a reasonable settlement of the Ulster problem. But the British Unionist party was equally perplexed by the idea of an Ulster solution. Andrew Bonar Law, the Unionist leader, was deeply committed to the Ulster Unionist cause, but he had a party to lead and to keep together and this party was divided about what it was supposed to be fighting for. As one Unionist put it 'If we go for compromise on Ulster, we desert the rest of Ireland, but avoid civil war: is it right for the sake of avoiding civil war to ignore the loyalists in the South and West of Ireland?' (quoted in Williamson, 1988, p. 72).

Other Unionists held that the primary objective was anyway to defend the integrity of the United Kingdom above the interests of any Unionist section in Ireland. And the Unionists were convinced that they had the Liberals at a disadvantage over Ireland; they did not want compromise, they wanted victory, and revenge for the three electoral defeats of 1906 and 1910.

While the party raged in England, war was prepared in Ireland. Threats of resistance had failed to issue in any organized shape in 1886 and 1893, but now the Ulster Unionists moved to place themselves on a military footing. In January 1912 some Unionists began openly to drill and train; they were able to keep within the law by obtaining the sanction of a magistrate, since they claimed to be rendering citizens more effective for the defence of the constitution. A year later the standing committee of the Ulster Unionist Council announced that the time had come to unite volunteers into one military force, and the Ulster Volunteer Force (UVF) was founded, with a headquarters staff and a network of regiments and battalions, with supporting units. Altogether some 90,000 men were recruited, one English newspaper describing them as 'of the finest class' (Buckland, 1973, pp. 58–9).

But such tactics need not be the prerogative of Ulster Unionists. Just as Unionists could claim that they were a community with a right to resist home rule by force of arms, so the nationalists could reply that they were a community with the right to insist upon home rule by force of arms. In November 1913, in response to an article entitled 'The North Began', written by Eoin MacNeill, one of the founders of the Gaelic League, nationalists began to organize an Irish volunteer force, based on the same principles as the one in the north: local regiments, drilling sessions, a headquarters command. This organization, its founders emphasized, was not created to fight the UVF, nor was it in existence to fight the British; it was simply there to defend home rule. And home rule seemed to need defending, as Redmond's acceptance of even the minor concession agreed by the Liberal cabinet – the county option offered in March 1914, a kind of plebiscite to ascertain which Ulster counties might be temporarily retained under direct Westminster rule – was regarded by nationalists as tantamount to failure.

The crux of the Ulster problem lay not only in the determined resistance of Unionist Ulster, but in the very nature of the province itself. Ulster was not, as Unionists liked to claim, a 'Protestant province'. In the pre-war years Ulster returned thirty-three MPs, sixteen Unionists and seventeen Nationalists and Liberals. Unionists could not even claim to control a solid bloc of Ulster seats, for their eastern strength was separated from their western constituencies by the nationalist seats of Mid, North and East Tyrone. Southern Ulster was mainly nationalist; so was the north-west. Belfast had the strongly nationalist West Belfast constituency. As so often in Irish politics, the evidence for special treatment was far from clear-cut, but the case for special treatment of Ulster Unionists could hardly be resisted. This in turn meant that the Protestants of the south and west must be left to their own fate, but their influence, though electorally negligible, was still significant in the British Unionist party, where many of them, Lord Lansdowne, Lord Midleton and the like, held positions of eminence. Carson, too, was reluctant to give up the fight for all Ireland, though he also acknowledged that it might yet come to a settlement that saved Ulster, or some of it, for government Ministers were by 1913 and 1914 making statements that Ulster could only obtain some special treatment for herself; she could not stand in the way of the rest of Ireland.

The Liberal government, threshing around for some positive options, found itself in further difficulties when, in March 1914, it became embroiled in a controversy over the possible use of military force in Ulster. On 14 March Winston Churchill declared that there were worse things in politics than bloodshed, and that force would be met with force. A special Cabinet committee then proceeded to take what were, allegedly, preventative measures, in the expectation of a clash between the Crown forces and the UVF. To some cavalry officers stationed at the Curragh Camp near Dublin this looked like a preparation for full-scale coercion. It was certainly provocative in their eyes (Morgan, 1991, p. 142). The commander-in-chief in Ireland, Sir Arthur Paget, feared that some of his officers would prove disaffected, especially since a number of them had homes in Ulster. The War Office agreed that such officers constituted a special case, and that they should be allowed to remain behind, but that any other officers would be dismissed the service if they refused to go north. Paget compounded the difficulties by giving his commanders the impression that moves were afoot that would create 'intense excitement' and that conflict with the UVF was imminent. He then declared that anyone who did not feel that he could obey orders in this eventuality need not attend a second conference to be held that afternoon: thus, officers seemed to be given the alternative of doing their duty in Ulster or being dismissed. Brigadier Hubert Gough and officers of his cavalry brigade declared they preferred dismissal if they were to be made to undertake operations against the UVF. Gough managed to extract from the War Office a promise that he and his fellow officers would not be employed to coerce Ulster into the acceptance of the Home Rule Bill. The War Minister, J. E. B. Seely, added another concession: while the government retained the right to use the army to maintain law and order it had 'no intention whatever of taking advantage of this right to crush political opposition to the policy or principles of the Home Rule Bill'. Field Marshal Lord French, believing that this was the Cabinet's view, further conceded to Gough that under no circumstances would the troops be used to 'enforce the present Home Rule Bill on Ulster' (Jalland, 1980, pp. 229–33).

On 25 March Asquith repudiated these concessions; but the government had clearly forfeited any possibility of using force to bring the Ulster Unionists to heel. In truth, this would have been a risky enterprise. British public opinion would have disliked the spectacle of British soldiers forcing home rule on a reluctant people at the point of the bayonet, though it is possible that, once the shooting started, then the government

85

would simply have had to go through with the unpleasant task of applying military force in a liberal democracy.

Developments in Ireland seemed to be moving the crisis beyond a democratic solution anyway. On 24–25 April 1914 the Ulster Unionists successfully completed a daring enterprise by smuggling 35,000 rifles and five million rounds of ammunition from Germany into Larne harbour. The cabinet considered moving against the Unionists, but acknowledged the difficulty involved in prosecuting such large numbers of what it called the 'representative Ulster "rabble"' (Jalland, 1980, p. 246). Instead they pursued the idea of 'county option', but they were so obviously at a disadvantage that the Unionist opposition felt no need to concede – even if such a concession had been acceptable to the Ulster Unionists (which it was not) and to those Unionists who held that the fight was for the United Kingdom and Ireland, not just Ulster counties. A conference at Buckingham Palace on 21–4 July ended in deadlock; two days later the Irish Volunteers emulated the UVF and landed 1,500 rifles at Howth, County Dublin. Four people were killed and thirty-seven wounded when troops, harassed and provoked, opened fire on a crowd at Bachelor's Walk. Now the government appeared to be using the force against Nationalists that it declined to employ against its Unionist enemies. On 1 August more Irish Volunteer guns were landed in County Wicklow. Civil war was averted by the United Kingdom's declaration of war against Germany on 4 August.

There can be no doubt that Irish nationalism became more militant as a direct response to Ulster Unionist resistance to the third home-rule bill. But it is important to realize that in Catholic Ireland nationalism had by 1914 become the dominant and driving force in its own right. It was no longer driven by land hunger or material grievances; indeed, by 1914 Ireland was enjoying the benefits of membership of the United Kingdom with fewer of the disadvantages than ever before. The importance of nationalism was seen in the last place where it might have been expected to be encountered: the labour movement. In 1913 James Connolly and James Larkin led a strike of the Irish Transport and General Workers Union against the

Dublin employers, whose spokesman, William Martin Murphy, was a prominent home ruler. A bitter conflict ensued, in which the Dublin Metropolitan Police played a leading and controversial role, baton-charging strikers on 30 and 31 August and causing serious injuries and one death. The following November an Irish Citizen Army was founded to protect strikers against the police and to provide a force to oppose the employers. It was of no significance in the strike. But it was refounded and quickly politicized into a nationalist conspiracy. One of its leading members and supporters, the dramatist Sean O'Casey, watched with dismay as James Connolly led the ICA into a conjunction with the Irish Volunteers and Sinn Fein, and 'Irish Labour lost a leader.' O'Casey was a hostile observer, for he had a deep distaste for what he regarded as bourgeois nationalism; nevertheless, his observations on Connolly were not far off the mark. Connolly was a Marxist, and saw British rule as synonymous with capitalism. But he had also imbibed the culture of Irish Catholic nationalism (even if he had, possibly, rejected its religious faith) and his Marxism became more abstract as his nationalism asserted itself. Ulster Unionists who happened to be working-class as well were, in his view, deluded, and were no longer to be considered members of the 'Irish nation' (Morgan, 1991, pp. 168–78). In September 1914 Connolly met the Supreme Council of the Irish Republican Brotherhood in order to plan a rising before the end of the war. Patrick Pearse, a schoolmaster, Gaelic Leaguer, and now an advocate of freedom through violence, was present, as were other nationalists whose names, then unknown, were soon to be emblazoned over Ireland during the 1916 Easter Rising in Dublin.

Any such prospect seemed remote in the early period of the Great War. At the outbreak of war John Redmond pledged that Ireland would, through the joint efforts of the UVF and the Irish Volunteers, defend her own shores, and in September 1914 he won a significant concession from Asquith, whose prevarication seemed endless, when the Cabinet agreed, under pressure, to place the third home-rule bill on the statute book, with its implementation delayed until the end of the war and a promise of an amending bill to deal with the Ulster question. This latter provision might be regarded as ominous, for Redmond at least, but he saw his role as one of leading nationalist Ireland into the empire, gaining the goodwill and admiration of Great Britain, and perhaps even reaching a measure of agreement with the Ulster Unionists, all by means of Irish nationalist participation in the war. On 20 September 1914 he followed up a speech he had made in the Commons by urging Irish Volunteers to enlist in England's war. This provoked a split in the movement, with a minority calling themselves still by the name 'Irish Volunteers', and the vast majority who followed Redmond adopting the title 'National Volunteers'. Redmond, undaunted, followed up his pro-war and pro-recruitment speeches with a declaration at Kilkenny on 17 October that 'the Union of 1800 is dead . . . we have won at last a free constitution' (Doherty and Hickey, 1989, p. 182).

Nationalist enthusiasm for the war faltered, as did British enthusiasm, under the onslaught of high casualty lists. In Ireland there were also doubts of a more fundamental kind, even if they were only expressed by a small minority as yet. In May 1915 Sir Edward Carson and eight other Unionists entered the government when Asquith responded to criticism of his war leadership by forming a coalition. John Redmond was offered a place in the Cabinet, but, following the policy laid down by Parnell of no nationalist acceptance of British office, he declined. But these rebuffs, if that is what they were, were offset by nationalist Ireland's benefits from the war. Farmers did well by selling cattle to the British market; wives and families of serving soldiers received state allowances. It was not nationalist Ireland's desire to abandon England's war, but its readiness to support the conflict (albeit with reservations) that provoked the separatists to go ahead with their conspiracy, which, in January 1916, they finally decided to stage no later than Easter. The military council of the IRB met in secret with James Connolly, who was co-opted. The Irish-American organization, Clan na Gael, was alerted that weapons would be required, and on 9 March it informed Pearse that guns would arrive from Germany during 23–5 April. On 3 April Patrick Pearse issued orders for Volunteer manoeuvres to begin on Saturday 23 April. On 6 April, Easter Sunday was finally selected as the date for the rising and on 8 April Pearse's new orders for manoeuvres on Easter Sunday were approved by Eoin MacNeill, only to be countermanded when he realized that he himself was the victim of a conspiracy by the ringleaders of the rising to dupe him into the belief that the British planned to disarm nationalist organizations. This caused confusion among the Volunteers, and when the appointed day arrived, on 24 April, only a minority of Irish Volunteers, together with the Irish Citizen Army, turned out.

The rebels had bungled, yet their rising was a turning-point in the history of modern Ireland. They held out for only a week, and sporadic fighting outside Dublin was easily suppressed by the Crown forces, but their stand for freedom caught the imagination of nationalist Ireland. The British army shot only thirteen rebel ringleaders; yet those thirteen had their names entered into the nationalist catechism, while the 'other half-million' who served in France and Gallipoli, and wherever the firing line extended, were soon forgotten. The rebels fought for an independent Ireland, yet nothing contributed more to the partition of their country, as Ulster Unionists gained the advantage of loyalty to Britain in the war, and Irish nationalists forfeited all benefits from their participation in the conflict. The rebels did this, not only because of their brave stand, but because they became martyrs in a popular nationalist tradition that had been taught – even by John Redmond and his home rulers – to venerate martyrdom for Ireland (though not to emulate it). Their Catholicism came to the fore and the Church could not condemn the rebels (as according to its own precepts it should have done) because their deaths turned public disapproval into sympathy and because these men were not godless Fenians but, on the contrary, very devout men who died for a holy Ireland, a Gaelic Ireland and a free Ireland. Above all, the rebels made nationalism into a kind of moral force: freedom was more important than any other consideration and moderation in its cause was not a virtue. This rendered any genuine contact with Ulster Unionists impossible. Compromise was not a word that nationalism could value, and Ulster Unionists, themselves opposed to any all-Ireland settlement, were more than ready to meet intransigence with intransigence. There was not much room for manoeuvre between the Ulster Covenant of 1913 and the proclamation of the republic of 1916.

And yet compromise had to be sought, at least by the British government, which found Ireland a distraction from the main business of winning the war. In May–June 1916 Lloyd George negotiated with Redmond and Carson for a settlement, based on the exclusion of six Ulster counties, but his plan foundered on the ambiguity over the permanence or otherwise of partition, which British and southern Irish Unionists exposed as a way of discrediting Lloyd George's (admittedly devious) tactics. In April 1917 the government, spurred on by the United States of America's decision to enter the war on the allied side, tried again; and a convention of leading Irishmen, Unionist and Nationalist, was assembled to see if it could create its own solution. Sinn Fein boycotted the convention and there seemed good reason now for the home rule party to fear its adversaries. Between February and August 1917 Sinn Fein challenged the parliamentary party in a series of by-elections, and won four victories, including the highly symbolic triumph of a survivor from the Easter Rising, Eamon de Valera, in County Clare. De Valera campaigned in Clare in July 1917 wearing his Volunteer uniform, but paying a necessary and pious obeisance to Ireland's great Catholic nationalist past, for Clare was where emancipation was fought for and won in 1828.

Between 1917 and 1918 the central struggle was not between England and Ireland, nor even between Nationalist Ireland and Unionist Ireland, but between home rulers and Sinn Fein, with the militant movement, based on the Irish Volunteers, watching the antics of all politicians with a suspicious and jaundiced eye. The Irish Convention seemed to vindicate those who held that nothing was to be gained from any British plans for Irish home rule, yet it did witness an important breakthrough, when an influential group of southern Irish Unionists, led by Lord Midleton, reached agreement with the nationalists over a scheme for Irish self-government. But the Convention's report, carried on 5 April, was signed by less than half its members; and its deliberations were rendered irrelevant by the greatest crisis of the war, when German armies threatened to break through on the western front in March 1918, and the government decided that it must take powers to introduce conscription into Ireland.

The government was hard-pressed for manpower; it was also influenced by the recognition that, as one of its supporters put it, 'England, Scotland and Wales would not have stood a call on men up to 50, if Ireland was still left with her young men unconscripted' (Williamson, 1988, p. 129). But nothing could have been more damaging to the home rule party's attitude to the war, already compromised by the Easter Rising. John Redmond died on 6 March 1918, with John Dillon assuming the leadership of the party. On 9 April Lloyd George introduced a military service bill to apply to Ireland, and the home rulers showed their impotence by walking out of the House, thus vindicating by their actions the policy advocated by Arthur Griffith, who had always held that nothing was to be gained by attending the Westminster Parliament. The home rulers joined with Sinn Fein, the Catholic Church, and other nationally minded bodies in an anti-conscription campaign that frequently resembled a Catholic moral crusade rather than a political pro-test. On 19 April a home rule candidate withdrew from a by-election in King's County to signify the party's objection to conscription; the Sinn Fein candidate was returned unopposed, once again emphasizing Sinn Fein's leading role in the campaign. On 23 April a one-day strike called by nationalists was successful everywhere except in Unionist Ulster, which again branded nationalists as traitors to the British cause in the war. Meanwhile the authorities found themselves obliged to move against those found in possession of arms in Clare, Galway and Tipperary, and in May the Cabinet, with its discredited policy of combining conscription with the enactment of a home rule bill as a sweetener, announced a German plot to incite insurrec-tion in Ireland. This enabled it to substitute a military for a political policy, and in June home rule and conscription plans were abandoned, though Ireland continued to supply at least a steady trickle of volunteers for the British army.

This was a sad and confusing end to the high hopes entertained by Redmond and Asquith in August 1914, when nationalist Ireland entered the greatest war in British history. Its consequences were soon to be revealed in the general election which followed the armistice of 11 November 1918. In December 1918 Ireland went to the polls in the first election held under a mass democratic franchise. Sinn Fein campaigned on the ambiguous agenda which it had drawn up in an Ard Fheis held in October 1917: that is, it aimed at winning recognition by the international community for the Irish Republic, and would then allow the people to choose by referendum their own form of government. The flaws in this document, and especially its relegation of democratic opinion to a secondary role, might have been exploited by the home rulers, and the party did its best to carry the fight to the enemy. But they were shackled to the disasters of their wartime policy, and especially damaged by the conscription crisis. Irish soldiers still in France might have been more sympathetic to the home rulers, but they were not allowed facilities to vote from abroad. Sinn Fein fought on the issue of 'national independence' and it was helped in its single-issue campaign by the Irish Labour Party's decision not to contest the election. They conducted a campaign that combined the best of the new and the traditional. Sinn Fein did not truckle to Westminster; but it also claimed to stand in the great tradition of Charles Stewart Parnell and the real nationalism that he upheld in his prime. Sinn Fein did not advocate violence, yet it indicated approval of the men of 1916, and Irish Volunteers campaigned on its behalf. On Ulster, however, its traditionalism was unhelpful, to say the least. One Sinn Feiner announced that they were not going to coerce the minority, but 'they were not going to allow the minority to coerce them, because no minority would be allowed to stand between them and the destiny of the Irish nation' (*Cork Examiner*, 19 November 1918).

The results of this, the first democratic election in Ireland, were symptomatic of the special conditions under which Irish democracy operated in 1918. Sinn Fein was unopposed in twenty-five constituencies, by no means a new phenomenon in

Irish elections, for in the late nineteeth century uncontested seats were common enough, reflecting as they did the fact that the home-rule party was, in many areas, the Catholic party for the Catholic people: now Sinn Fein fitted that image. Sinn Fein won only 48 per cent of the vote in Ireland as a whole but 65 per cent in what later became the twenty-six-county independent Irish state. But the British first past the post system gave Sinn Fein a total of seventy-three seats, with the Irish parliamentary party winning only six. Unionists won twenty-five seats, and independent Unionists won one seat. Nationalist Ireland stubbornly retained its foothold in Ulster, helped by a compromise between home rulers and Sinn Feiners arranged by the Roman Catholic bishops – another sign of the nature of democracy in Ireland. But if Ulster was by no means all Unionist, then Ireland was by no stretch of the imagination all nationalist. Yet de Valera described Ulster Unionism as 'a thing of the mind only, non-existent in the world of reality' (Buckland, 1981, p. 18).

Sinn Fein was more successful in the rural than in the urban districts, for the bulk of recruitment for the British army in the war came from the cities and towns; farmers' sons were less willing to serve. Sinn Fein also took a greater share of the younger vote, following the 1918 franchise reforms, but it was by no means the obvious party of the young, and the home rulers gained 15 per cent of the votes of males recorded as being aged between 14 and 24 in the 1911 census, against Sinn Fein's 17 per cent (Garvin, 1981, p. 121). The home rulers were not 'swept away' in 1918. Ireland still did not speak with one voice, even in nationalist areas. Unionist Ulster stood on its guard in 1918 as it had done in every home-rule crisis since 1886. The conflict between Unionism and nationalism was about to be renewed. It remained to be seen if the British government would or could insist upon a settlement.

7

The Division of the Spoils, 1919–1923

The aftermath of the Great War was an unlikely background for a settlement of the Irish question as it now posed itself. The British government was immediately immersed in serious foreign and domestic issues: the Versailles Peace Conference, reconstruction, a wave of industrial unrest. Ireland was indeed listed in the programme on which the Lloyd George Conservative and Liberal coalition went to the country: 'So long as the Irish question remains unsettled there can be no political peace either in the United Kingdom or in the Empire, and we regard it as one of the first obligations of British statesmanship to explore all practical paths towards the settlement of this grave and difficult question, on the basis of self-government' (Quoted in Boyce, 1972, p. 25).

But there was no incentive to fulfil this obligation, and one of the most important consequences of British delay was that it left a political vacuum which, it must be said, Sinn Fein did not fill. Sinn Fein adopted its policy of refusing to go to Westminster, constituting itself Dáil Éireann (the parliament of Ireland) in Dublin in January 1919, and looking to what one of its supporters called the 'irresistible' power of passive resistance (O'Hegarty, 1919, p. 25). It also appealed for recognition to the Versailles Peace Conference, which it seems seriously to have believed would meet Irish nationalist claims. None of these tactics bore fruit: the British ignored Dáil Éireann; there was no widespread manifestation of passive resistance; and the Peace Conference set aside Sinn Fein's appeal. The policy of abstention from the British House of Commons was proving as futile as the Irish parliamentary party always claimed it would be.

This had serious consequences for nationalist Ireland, and indeed for Ireland as a whole and for Great Britain. A vote for Sinn Fein in the general election of 1918 was not a vote for a war of independence, but it was a sign to those who wanted to use force that the country had rejected British rule, and a military campaign against British rule could run in tandem with (and yet not be controlled by) the political campaign of Sinn Fein. The Irish Volunteers had no intention of dancing to any politician's tune; they were already looking forward to an attack upon anyone who, in their estimate, gave aid and succour to the British civilian or soldier. Such a person must be 'destroyed with the least possible delay'. And if a renewed campaign of violence failed, then the movement could again go underground and await another favourable opportunity (Townshend, 1983, p. 320). The Irish Republican Army, as it now began to call itself, was given a sense of its moral superiority by incidents such as the death of volunteer Thomas Ashe in September 1917, following his hunger strike and forced feeding. Martyrs were as useful to them as soldiers; but it was with a hard-headed realism that they now began to engage the enemy, chiefly the Royal Irish Constabulary. On 19 January 1919, two days before the first meeting of the Dáil, volunteers ambushed and killed two policemen in County Tipperary. This was by no means a popular action; and the Volunteers encouraged each other with the reflection that the people might not understand at first what the IRA was trying to achieve on their behalf, but no doubt would do so in the end (Kee, 1972, p. 632).

The British government had to meet violence with what it regarded as firmness, yet it had committed itself to the policy of granting some form of home rule to Ireland. This meant that it was unable, even if it was willing, to recognize a state of war in Ireland and set about the systematic reconquest of the country. It needed a holding operation, until such time as it could induce nationalist Ireland to accept whatever the British had in mind to offer. The government made its own task more difficult by proclaiming Dáil Éireann as an illegal organization in August 1919. Now that nationalist politicians were deprived of a legal institution, the government could, it believed, tackle violence. But it was reluctant to go beyond a reconstruction of the police force, or to declare martial law. This might have proved effective if indeed the police force had been properly equipped, reinforced, and its morale raised. But the government resolved in December 1919 to try to increase the force through the expedient of recruiting extra men from ex-servicemen enlisted in Great Britain. In July 1920 another set of reinforcements, the Auxiliary Division (composed of ex-officers) was raised and sent in companies of a hundred to the most disturbed areas. This force soon became notorious for its bravery and its reckless behaviour. It was rivalled in its indiscipline by the new recruits to the ordinary RIC, known as 'Black and Tans' after their mixed military and police uniforms, and within a short time the forces of law and order were themselves the centre of controversy concerning their own lawlessness – a controversy played upon by the IRA's propaganda machine, since it shifted attention away from the IRA's own ruthless campaign. As one ex-Black and Tan put it, 'We had some tough looking hands; it was a case of who got the first shot in.' And while the regular RIC 'didn't like it' and 'weren't fond of them', the reputation of the force as a whole suffered. No longer could it behave as a police force, policing Ireland on behalf of the civilian; rather, it looked more and more like an army of occupation (Brewer, 1990, pp. 104, 112–16). The warlike nature of the conflict became even more obvious when in December 1920 the government proclaimed martial law in the south-west, a policy which again earned it criticism for heavy-handed methods, without any benefits that might come from a full application of martial law everywhere (Townshend, 1983, p. 354).

The government was influenced in its decision by the knowledge that it must seek a political settlement in Ireland, and that it must do so soon. By the end of 1919 the government had to find an Irish policy, since the conclusion of peace treaties in Europe meant that the 1914 Government of Ireland Act must come into effect, barring a substitute. The Cabinet was sensitive to the influence of American opinion, and to the mood abroad which favoured self-determination for small nations. In 1920 it devised another home rule bill, this time one which was aimed at satisfying both Irish nationalists and Ulster Unionists, and thus resolving the crisis that had immobilized the Liberal Cabinet in the summer of 1914.

The Government of Ireland Bill was introduced into the House of Commons in February 1920 and passed through Parliament by the following December. It created two states in Ireland, both endowed with almost complete power in internal matters, but with few fiscal powers and only very limited taxation capacity. Each state had a House of Commons elected on proportional representation, and a senate, elected on a high property qualification in the south to give representation to minorities, but elected in the north on proportional representation mainly by the Commons. The government was guided in its home-rule policy by two central concerns: its belief that it must acknowledge the reality of Ulster Unionism and a lively sense of self-interest, for in establishing two Parliaments in Ireland, instead of merely excluding the north and leaving it under Westminster, it ensured that the world would not accuse it of seeking to govern any nationalists in Ireland against their will (Ulster Unionists would enjoy that doubtful privilege).

The government was at pains to declare that it did not intend partition to be permanent. It created a Council of Ireland, consisting of a president to be nominated by the Crown on the advice of the government, and forty representatives, half nominated by each of the Irish Parliaments. This council would deal with matters of common concern, and its powers could be widened by agreement between the two Irish parliaments. It would provide both a practical and a symbolic link between north and south, and, as a Conservative party pamphlet argued, it 'provides that there shall be *one* Parliament in Ireland whenever Ireland herself agrees . . . This is real self-determination since it is founded on agreement, and is not a sham union requiring force and coercion to keep it in existence' (Conservative Party, Harvester Press Microfiche, 1921/6).

The government did not ask itself whether or not its policy of obliging southern Ireland to accept its Home Rule Bill amounted to a kind of sham as well, but it had more immediate problems in devising its policy for the north. Partition, however defined, left minorities behind in the new states. The southern Protestant minority must, in the nature of things, be very small, however southern Ireland was delimited. But the size of the northern, Catholic minority was a matter of more vital concern to the new Northern Ireland state. The British government was aware of this, and aware too of its responsibilities to Ulster nationalists, for it initially sought to establish a nine-county Northern Ireland, only to reduce the area to six counties when Ulster Unionists protested that they would not undertake to work the Act unless they were given only those areas which they could reasonably hope to control: Antrim, Armagh, Down, Fermanagh, Londonderry and Tyrone. Even these contained significant local nationalist communities, with one-third of the population of the new state unreconciled to its existence.

Ulster Unionists did not vote for the bill as it passed through the House; but they knew that it was the best that they could expect. And, as Captain Charles Craig, brother of the Ulster Unionist leader Sir James, put it, 'We see our safety, therefore, in having a Parliament of our own, for we believe that once a Parliament is set up and working well . . . we should fear no one, and we feel that we would then be in a position of absolute security' (Kennedy, 1988, p. 58).

Ulster Unionists felt that they had much need of that security. In 1920 the IRA campaign began to take serious effect in the north, and the fact that it was launched from Catholic districts increased Unionist fury, which was vented on Catholics irrespective of their involvement in the terror. Catholics were excluded from their places of work in Belfast. Sinn Fein added to the general tension by instituting a boycott of Belfast goods, partly as a response to the 'Partition Act', but also to demonstrate to the north that it could bring Unionist business to its knees. The Belfast troubles gave further incentive to Sinn Fein to retaliate with a boycott, and despite some opposition (for example, from the northerner Ernest Blythe, who warned his

98

fellow Sinn Fein MPs that the boycott 'would destroy for ever the possibility of any union') it was rigidly enforced. The British government showed a total lack of concern about the effects of the boycott on northern industry, thus reinforcing the Ulster Unionist perception that they had better look after themselves (Johnson, 1981, pp. 287–307). This feeling was enhanced by the British government's decision to raise and arm what was in effect the remains of the old UVF in the form of a special constabulary. This force was exclusively Protestant, and came to be seen by nationalists as the worst example of Unionist partiality and violence. But it undoubtedly reduced the regular army's commitment in the north, and placed the largest responsibility for the restoration of law and order on Ulster Unionists themselves (Buckland, 1979, pp. 180–1).

P. S. O'Hegarty, one of Sinn Fein's most idealistic thinkers, described the impact of the economic boycott on Irish politics: 'it was merely a blind and suicidal contribution to the general hate' (Johnson, 1981, p. 307). But the 'general hate', the war of terror and revenge throughout Ireland, had important implications for British government policy. The actions of the Crown forces, especially of the Black and Tans and Auxiliaries, reflected badly on the British government, which found itself criticized, not only by international opinion but by an influential section of its own public, including some, like the Archbishop of Canterbury, whose integrity could not be doubted. But until the spring of 1921 the Cabinet felt that it had no option but to stand its ground and meet war with war. Nevertheless, it ruminated on the possibilities of some initiatives, while fearing that, as Lloyd George himself put it, 'Supposing you got a truce and negotiations. To make them succeed you'd have to pay too much and if you didn't they'd fail' (Middlemass, 1971, p. 68). The government still felt that it must first achieve a military victory. But in May 1921 it was receiving unfavourable reports from Ireland not only of the prospects of victory but of the poor morale and fighting capacity of its troops (Ibid., p. 71).

Nevertheless, at least one part of the home-rule policy was coming to life. In May the election campaign for the first Northern Ireland Parliament began, with Ulster Unionists being

99

warned that 'we are now masters of our own fate ... Great Britain has acknowledged to the full our oft-attested claim to be regarded as a free and independent people, under the Union Jack' (Kennedy, 1988, p. 57). Sir James Craig also appealed to Unionists to remember that 'we have to govern not you and me, but the whole people of this province' (Ibid., p. 59). He won the election with a predictable, yet resounding, victory; and when the first Northern Ireland Parliament was opened by the King in Belfast on 22 June 1921 he made an appeal that 'every man of Irish birth, whatever be his creed and wherever be his home, should work in loyal cooperation with the free communities on which the British Empire is based.' This draft of the King's speech had been seen and approved by the Cabinet; but the pressure on the government to seek peace was increasing, not only from the king, but from the statesmen of the empire, who were meeting in London in the Imperial Conference. As Lord Birkenhead put it, the speech was in 'harsh disparity' with one he had made on the same day, declaring that the British would continue the war. The South African Prime Minister, Field Marshal Jan Smuts, acted as intermediary between the Cabinet and Sinn Fein, and on 8 July the government finally agreed to seek a truce (Middlemass, III, pp. 77–85), which finally came into effect on 11 July. The truce was a measure both of the IRA's success and of its failure. It had brought the British to the point where they felt that they must negotiate before applying military force to the fullest extent, but, as Michael Collins wrote:

> We had prevented the enemy so far from defeating us. We had not, however, succeeded in getting the government entirely into our hands, and we had not succeeded in beating the British out of Ireland, militarily ... We had reached in July last the high-water mark of what we could do in the way of economic and military resistance. (Hopkinson, 1988, p. 9)

Shortly after the truce was arranged, negotiations began between the British government and Sinn Fein.

The first difficulty was to discover a formula by which the British and Irish could meet and discuss terms. Lloyd George would not accept any basis other than Irish membership of the empire; Sinn Fein rejected this, though de Valera stated his 'recommendation' that the Irish could accept a 'certain treaty of free association with the British Commonwealth group' to meet the objections of the 'present dissenting minority' – the Ulster Unionists. But the pressure to persevere was strong, and in the end Lloyd George found a form of words which enabled serious negotiations to begin. On 29 September he offered talks to ascertain 'how the association of nations known as the British Empire may best be reconciled with Irish national aspirations', which the Irish accepted the following day. Lloyd George laid down the British terms throughout the negotiations: dominion status on the Canadian model, with certain strategic and defence safeguards arising from Ireland's proximity to Great Britain. These were the conditions which were, in substance, accepted by Arthur Griffith and Michael Collins in December. But the talks were prolonged because the Irish, having accepted an invitation which demanded compromise of the republican ideal, then sought a means of modifying the British offer, or even rejecting it on the grounds that it did not apply to a united Ireland. These tactics, even if skilfully played, might, at best, have ended in a reluctant British withdrawal from the talks. They could not have budged Lloyd George from his fundamental terms, for the government had the military force to fall back upon, and a public opinion that would, albeit reluctantly, have supported its government, support which it denied in the Black and Tan war. But the Irish position, never strong, was further weakened by their own internal divisions. Arthur Griffith never found dominion status unacceptable. Collins, though a member of the IRB, was a pragmatic politician who saw his task as one of making the best terms he could for his people. De Valera was a subtle politician, who hoped to find a means of reconciling republican status with dominion status, but this – though it later came to pass as empire evolved further into commonwealth – was constitutionally unacceptable to the British in 1921.

De Valera's determination to control the negotiations from

Dublin further complicated matters. He was not part of the delegation and was not subject to the pressures, emotions and perspectives that Griffith, Collins and their colleagues experienced. Griffith was prepared to play the Ulster card, as the Irish agreed they would, demanding a united Ireland or a greater measure of independence. But when he did so, in November, he only gave the British a further advantage, for Lloyd George obtained from Griffith a promise that, if the British Prime Minister were to defend his negotiations against a right-wing Unionist backlash, then Griffith would agree to a boundary commission to revise the boundaries of the Northern Ireland state (Boyce, 1972, pp. 168–9). Lloyd George succeeded in carrying the Unionist party with him; but his pressure on Sir James Craig to exchange the sovereignty of Westminster for that of Dublin was rejected indignantly by the Northern Ireland Prime Minister. Yet too much can be made of Lloyd George's subterfuge. The fact was that, in 1921 as in 1914, Ulster Unionists formed a solid and unmoving resistance to Dublin rule. The Irish had either to accept that fact or try to challenge it by the use of force – force which only brought failure, and increasing bitterness between Catholic and Protestant in the north. It is not surprising, then, that after the Ulster Unionist rejection of Lloyd George's plan in November, the talks moved forward on the assumption that, for the time being at least, Northern Ireland would not be an integral part of any settlement. On 1 December the British delegation made its final offer of a draft treaty. The Cabinet in Dublin was divided, but decided to reject the terms and put the blame on Ulster. Back in London Lloyd George was ready to move in for the final phase in the talks. He swept aside the rather unconvincing attempts by Griffith to make a break on Ulster, reminding him of his promise made in November not to let Lloyd George down on the Ulster issue, and warning the Irish of the dire consequences of rejection: immediate and terrible war. The threat of war would not have carried such decisive weight had not Griffith and Collins already been more than halfway towards acceptance of the British terms. On 6 December 1921 they and the British delegates signed 'Articles of Agreement for a Treaty between Great Britain and Ireland'.

These articles gave Ireland dominion status on the Canadian model, with certain reservations concerning defence and British access to naval facilities. They were subject to ratification by both the British Parliament and the Parliament of 'southern Ireland' (those members elected under the Government of Ireland Act in May 1921). They were approved by both, though not without harsh words. In the House of Lords Sir Edward Carson launched a bitter attack on those in the Conservative party who had left his people, the southern Irish Protestants, in the lurch: England had reneged on her friends once again (Beckett, 1972, pp. 168–9). In Dublin the recriminations arose, not from the partition question, but on the 'betrayal' of the republican ideal, and the Irish delegation's acceptance of the British Crown as the symbol of Irish membership of the British Empire and Commonwealth (Boyce, 1991, pp. 327–8).

The treaty was signed on behalf of Great Britain and Ireland. Northern Ireland was not a party to it, though she was theoretically placed under Dublin jurisdiction, which she could petition the Crown to leave. If she did so, then a boundary commission would be appointed to ascertain how the frontier between north and south might be adjusted in accordance with the wishes of the inhabitants, but – a vital qualification – also taking into account economic and geographical considerations (Buckland, 1981, p. 38). This solution managed to reconcile the reality of partition with the imagination of unification. It saved the faces of southern nationalists, who had other matters to preoccupy them as opposition to the treaty became more decided, and those who signed the treaty were denounced as traitors. More ominously, the 'legion of the rearguard', the anti-treaty IRA, began to assert itself, and in many areas took over military and police installations now being handed over by the Crown forces.

The delegates who negotiated on behalf of Ireland did not include representatives from the northern Catholic minority (as it now was). Nor did they speak for the other Irish minority, the Protestants of the south. The former found their interests subordinated to the needs of the new Irish Free State, which had its priorities: the establishment of the new government's authority and the containment of the threat of civil war. Michael Collins was anxious to speak for northern Catholics, and frequently reminded the British government of its continuing responsibilities in the north, but his efforts were often counterproductive. In particular, his clandestine support for IRA activities in Northern Ireland (Hopkins, 1988, pp. 83–4) sat uneasily with his attempts to find a *rapprochement* with Sir James Craig to alleviate the condition of Ulster Catholics, who were all labelled Sinn Feiners by Unionists, and who, as a minority, paid the highest price in the communal strife that gripped Northern Ireland in the early months of 1922 (Buckland, 1979, pp. 194–205).

The southern Unionists were also set aside. They had played an important role in bringing about the truce in July 1921, thanks to Lord Midleton who, despite the murder of his nephew by the IRA, was prepared to put his country first. Unfortunately for them, their leaders put their trust in the British government, relying on Lloyd George to secure the best possible arrangements for their people. But the British Cabinet tended to think in wider terms of the empire and of Ireland's place within it: there was little concern for minority interests, or at least no over-riding concern for them. Thus the treaty contained no detailed provisions for a senate, which southern Unionists regarded as vital for their protection in the new Irish state, no provision for compensation for losses incurred in the recent troubles, and no provision for the completion of land purchase (Buckland, 1972, pp. 246–58). The old ascendancy must throw itself on the mercy of the new democracy and, while this democracy was by no means as hostile to the ascendancy as might have been expected, the southern minority was never allowed to live down its Unionism, or play any significant role in the politics or social formation of the Irish Free State. It would be a Catholic state for a Catholic people.

And the Northern state would be a Protestant state for a Protestant people. Sir James Craig declared his intention of making Northern Ireland into one of the finest examples of a democratic state. This would require the Unionist party to evolve two significant policy options in those areas where they were most subject to criticism: their treatment of the Roman Catholics and their overwhelmingly middle-class leadership which, it was held by some, stood in the way of their understanding of the needs of the working man. The Unionists made some headway in the latter. In 1918 they founded the Ulster Unionist Labour Association to express 'the views of labour unionists' (Buckland, 1973, pp. 138–43). But Unionist businessmen were reluctant to allow working men to play a leading role in the party, and some were hostile to taking up social issues. In local elections held in Belfast in 1920 Unionists performed badly, with their representation dropping from fifty-two to twenty-seven councillors. Thirteen labour representatives were returned (Buckland, 1973, p. 137). The lesson was clear: Unionists were on much safer ground when they played the Sinn Fein card. Even Sir Edward Carson, who was always aware of Unionist vulnerability on the social question, invariably concentrated his speeches on the anti-nationalist theme, warning that a Unionist who created 'disunion' (i.e. broke ranks and voted on other issues) was not a Unionist at all (Morgan, 1991, p. 221).

The Catholic question was the second vital issue. Ulster Unionists accepted and worked their state purely for their own security. Nevertheless, Sir James Craig frequently referred to the need to hold out the hand of friendship to the minority. But the early experience of the Northern Ireland state, the IRA's determined assault upon it, the fear held by many Protestants that all Catholics were involved in the conspiracy to strangle the new state at its birth, combined to add fuel to the already embittered feelings of Unionist and nationalist. It was tempting to play the sectarian card, especially as both the British and Irish governments seemed to be of one mind on at least one issue: the irksome nature of Ulster Unionism and its blind refusal to accept the 'broader' (i.e. Anglo-Irish) view of the Irish problem. And then there was the special character of the Northern Ireland state, with its small scale, highly local politics and the temptation, always strong and frequently irresistible, to make concessions to whatever vociferous group of Unionists

105

happened to stake a claim to government attention (Buckland, 1981, pp. 59–61).

In the north, democratic politics were mediated through these populist, sectarian and localized conditions; in the south, democracy itself had to fight for survival in the early life of the Free State. Here, the Dáil's approval of the Anglo-Irish Treaty in January 1922 by only sixty-four to fifty-seven votes placed the provisional government at a disadvantage. The issue of Free State versus Republic quickly became one of the democratic vote against the power of the gun, for the anti-treaty IRA refused to accept any political direction which, indeed, throughout the 'troubles' it had hardly known. Yet neither the new government nor its opponents relished the thought of civil war, and on 20 May 1922 Collins and de Valera negotiated a pact for elections which were to be held under the terms of the treaty to produce a new government for the Free State. Under the pact, the supporters and opponents of the treaty would stand as Sinn Fein candidates on a coalition basis, with numbers proportionate to existing strength in the Dáil. This pact was undermined by the British government's insistence that the new draft Irish constitution, prepared by the provisional government of the Free State, should conform to the terms of the treaty, especially in giving the Crown a genuine place in the constitution and in allowing judicial appeals to the British Privy Council. It broke down during the elections, as Collins realized that any hope of unity with the republicans had been destroyed by the monarchical style of the constitution (Hopkinson, 1988, pp. 105–10).

That the bulk of the nation wanted peace was shown in the elections: pro-treaty candidates won 239,195 votes, anti-treatyites 132,161 votes. But the real surprise was the 247,082 votes polled by other parties (Labour, independents, farmers), a sure sign that a large section – the largest of the three – wanted something more than the politics of abstract republicanism (or abstract dominion status). It was against this background, and with the moral support of the Roman Catholic Church, that the Free State government, after some hesitation, finally moved against the anti-treaty IRA. Yet the logic of that move was implicit in a statement made by the Free State Minister for Justice, Kevin O'Higgins: 'There are standing in the path today armed men saying to the massed men of this nation: you must not take a certain course. That is a position which never has been conceded in any democratic country. It will not be conceded here' (Townshend, 1983, p. 365).

The new state was shaken by the deaths, within ten days of each other, of its founders, Arthur Griffith, who died of a cerebral haemorrhage on 12 August 1922, and Michael Collins, who was killed in an ambush in County Cork. But W. T. Cosgrave and O'Higgins proved resolute in their defence of the state, and the government felt confident enough to allow the Dáil to meet in September 1922, when the new constitution was adopted.

Although the Free State government was prepared to use military force in order to defeat military challenge, it never lost control of its army, nor did its army seek to become in any sense the government of the country (Hopkins, 1988, p. 182). But as the war lengthened, and the government's promise of a quick victory receded, the state took more and more draconian measures, including executions under its Public Safety Act. There were, inevitably, atrocities on both sides. Kevin O'Higgins's father was shot dead at his home in February 1923. In March one of the worst incidents of the war occurred, when Free State soldiers tied eight republicans to a log and threw a mine among them. By now leading republicans were either rounded up or killed, and on 27 April de Valera offered to negotiate to end the war, an offer rejected by the government. By June 1923 de Valera acknowledged that the republicans had to endure what he called a 'victory . . . for the moment' of those who had 'destroyed the Republic' (Doherty and Hickey, 1989, p. 206).

By this time, too, the Northern Ireland government had achieved a degree of stability that at one time seemed beyond hope. But, again, this was at the cost of heavy security measures, a large police force, and special powers. Several Unionist MPs were quick to draw parallels between the events of 1922 and the history of 'massacres', such as those of 1641, which represented 'the spirit that animates the attack that is being made on Ulster today' (Kennedy, 1988, p. 98). In November 1922 the United Kingdom general election resulted in the return of eleven Unionists and two nationalists to Westminster. Northern Ireland nationalists ignored the poll, except in the two-seat constituency of Fermanagh and Tyrone. Mutual estrangement and bitterness, extending within as well as between Northern Ireland and the Irish Free State, marked the politics of the two new states of Ireland after peace was restored in 1923, and these feelings were to shape them both for generations.

8

Conclusion: Ascendancy and Democracy

When the historian surveys the history of Ireland between 1829 and 1923 he might be tempted, like Gibbon, to muse on the fact that he had witnessed the triumph, not of Christianity and barbarism, but of sectarianism and democracy. A British government imposed peace on Ireland in the aftermath of the 1798 rebellion. That peace enabled a central political force to emerge in the nineteenth century – the Roman Catholic democracy, strongly supported by the Catholic Church in Ireland and dedicated to the removal of numerous and various political and social disabilities, and, ultimately, to the achievement of a statehood (of whatever sort) that would enable it to enter its inheritance, its promised land. Charismatic figures emerged – O'Connell, Parnell, even for a time the Englishman Gladstone – who seemed to fulfil a role: that of Moses leading his people out of bondage. De Valera entered on that inheritance after 1932, once he acknowledged, as he at first signally failed to do, that (as the Catholic hierarchy put it) 'A Republic without popular recognition behind it is a contradiction in terms' (Doherty and Hickey, 1989, p. 203). This journey to the promised land was shaped and deeply influenced by the experience of being part of the United Kingdom, which was itself moving – slowly, and hardly ever consciously or directly, it must be emphasized – towards democratic government as the basis of its politics.

In 1828 Ireland was still in the grip of a small, mainly landowning, Protestant ascendancy. By 1914 that ascendancy had watched, almost helpless, as its power base was whittled away, mainly by a British state intent on securing the allegiance of Catholic Ireland through the means of dismantling the power of Protestant Ireland. But Protestant Ireland, though it accepted reforms, such as the disestablishment of its Church and land purchase, would not concede ultimate political power so easily. Reforms were swallowed, simply because there was no viable alternative and rebellion against the government conceding those reforms was impracticable and unreal. But home rule or any form of self-government was a different matter. The Irish, and especially the Ulster, Protestants drew the line there, and stood their ground. The southern Unionists, despite their considerable influence in the British Unionist party, had in the end to accept their fate, and see their ascendancy disappear in the new Catholic democracy placed over them in 1921; but the Ulster Unionists formed a community, with a region, and a determination to defend themselves and their land against the nationalists and their Liberal allies.

From this conflict there emerged a partitioned and self-governing Ireland, and two democracies deeply influenced by their sectarian origins. The machinery necessary to protect minorities – special voting registers, special blocking mechanisms in the legislatures, fundamentally entrenched rights – though embedded in political theory, were alien to the British, and therefore to the Irish political traditions: democracy meant majority rule, even if those majorities showed a disregard of the minority traditions, north and south. The localism so characteristic of Irish politics re-emerged in the two new states of Ireland, and the character of the Irish democracies was also shaped by the kind of local pressures which could be brought to bear on political parties, and on an Eamon de Valera as much as on a Sir James Craig. Finally, the presence in Ireland of violent and even anti-democratic organizations, though their influence must not be exaggerated, placed politicians at a disadvantage. Not only were their lives at risk; they were also deterred from abandoning established political positions for fear of offending the section of society from which these groups sprang. This problem diminished in the south, where de Valera blended Catholicism, republicanism and democracy through the institutions of the state, and marginalized militant challenges to its legitimacy. But in the north, with its large nationalist minority, the room for this kind of subtle political manoeuvre was much more restricted, and it was, in the event, attempted disastrously late.

Northern Ireland and the Irish Free State carried another significant characteristic forward from the period of the Union: their ideologies. Unionism and nationalism were forged under the conditions which British rule imposed on Ireland in the nineteenth century. Nationalism was the set of ideals and goals formulated by a people which saw itself as a subject nation; Unionism was the reaction to nationalism. The image of Ireland as a subject nation made nationalists appear more radical than they, or the vast majority of them, really were. The fact that Unionists sought to frustrate the march of a nation rendered their image more conservative than it was, and the need for community solidarity inhibited the voice of Liberal Unionism in the north. Nationalists set out to create a Gaelic, Catholic, economically self-sufficient, sovereign nation. Unionists set out with a steadfast determination not to be included in that nation. A democratically elected Catholic state in the south confronted a democratically elected Protestant state in the north. In each case 'democracy' was regarded as corresponding simply to the wishes of the majority. The essential elements of mutual trust and confidence between majority and minority were lacking in both states. This was the final, and wholly unforeseen, outcome of the British management of the transition from ascendancy to democracy in Ireland between 1828 and 1923.

References and Further Reading

An asterisk denotes works that are particularly useful for students

Beckett, J. C. 1966: *The Making of Modern Ireland, 1603–1923*. London.

—— 1972: *Confrontations: studies in Irish history*. London.

Bew, Paul 1978: *Land and the National Question in Ireland, 1858–1882*. Dublin.

* —— 1980: *Charles Stewart Parnell*. Dublin.

—— 1987: *Conflict and Conciliation in Ireland, 1890–1910*. Oxford.

Bowman, John 1982: *De Valera and the Ulster Question, 1917–1973*. Oxford.

Boyce, D. G. 1972: *Englishmen and Irish Troubles: British public opinion and the making of Irish policy, 1918–1922*. London.

—— 1988: *The Irish Question and British Politics, 1868–1986*. London.

—— 1989: Sir Edward Carson and Irish Unionism. In C. Brady (ed.), *Worsted in the Game: losers in Irish history*. Dublin. pp. 145–57.

* —— 1990: *Nineteenth Century Ireland: the search for stability*. Dublin.

* —— 1991: *Nationalism in Ireland*, new ed. London.

Brewer, John D. 1990: *The Royal Irish Constabulary: an oral history*. Belfast.

Bridgeman, William: *see* Williamson, P. (ed.).

Buckland, P. 1972: *Irish Unionism I: the Anglo-Irish and the new Ireland 1885–1922*. Dublin.

* —— 1973: *Irish Unionism II: Ulster Unionism and the origins of*

Northern Ireland, 1886–1922. Dublin.

—— 1979: *The Factory of Grievances: devolved government in Northern Ireland, 1921–1939*. Dublin.

—— 1981: *A History of Northern Ireland*. Dublin.

Butt, Isaac 1843: *Repeal of the Union*. Dublin.

—— 1847: *The Famine in the Land*. Dublin.

*Cairns, D., and Richards, S. 1988: *Writing Ireland: colonialism, nationalism and culture*. Manchester.

*Comerford, R. V. 1985: *The Fenians in context: Irish politics and society, 1848–1882*. Dublin.

Corish, P. J. 1967: *A History of Irish Catholicism*. Vol. V. Dublin.

*Daly, Mary E. 1986: *The Famine in Ireland*. Dublin.

Davis, A. (ed.) 1966: *Jonathan Swift: Irish Tracts, 1728–1733*. Oxford.

Davis, Richard 1974: *Arthur Griffith and Non-Violent Sinn Fein*. Dublin.

—— 1987: *The Young Ireland Movement*. Dublin.

Derry, J. W. 1976: *Castlereagh*. London.

Doherty, J. E., and Hickey, D. J. 1989: *A Chronology of Irish History since 1500*. Dublin.

Donnelly, J. S., Jnr. 1983: *Irish Peasants: violence and political unrest, 1780–1914*. Manchester.

Edwards, Owen Dudley 1988: *Eamon de Valera*. Cardiff.

Edwards, Owen Dudley, and Pyle, Fergus 1968: *1916: the Easter Rising*.

Edwards, Robin Dudley, and Williams, T. Desmond (eds.) 1956: *The Great Famine*. Dublin.

Edwards, Ruth Dudley 1977: *Patrick Pearse: the triumph of failure*. London.

Ervine, St John 1949: *Craigavon: Ulsterman*. London.

Farrell, Brian 1971: *The Founding of Dáil Éireann*. Dublin.

Fitzpatrick, David 1977: *Politics and Irish Life, 1913–1921: provincial experience of war and revolution*. Dublin.

—— 1986: *Ireland and the First World War*. Dublin.

Forester, Margery 1971: *Michael Collins: the lost leader*. London.

Gailey, Andrew 1987: *Ireland and the Death of Kindness: the experience of constructive Unionism*. Cork.

Gallagher, Michael 1979: The Pact Election of 1922. *Irish Historical Studies*, 21, no. 84, 404–21.

Garvin, Tom 1981: *The Evolution of Irish Nationalist Politics*. Dublin.

* —— 1987: *Nationalist Revolutionaries in Ireland, 1858–1928*. Oxford.

113

Geary, L. M. 1986: *The Plan of Campaign, 1886–1891*. Cork.

Gibbon, Peter 1975: *The Origins of Ulster Unionism: the formation of popular Protestant politics and ideology in nineteenth century Ireland.* Manchester.

Gladstone, W. E. *see* Matthew, H. G. C. (ed.).

Hobson, Bulmer (ed.) n.d.: *Letters of Theobald Wolfe Tone*. Dublin.

*Hopkinson, Michael 1988:*Green against Green: the Irish civil war.* Dublin.

*Hoppen, K. T. 1989: *Ireland since 1800*. London.

*Hutchinson, John 1987: *The Dynamics of Cultural Nationalism: the Gaelic Revival and the creation of the Irish nation state.* London.

Jackson, T. A. 1989: *The Ulster Party: Irish Unionism in the House of Commons, 1884–1911.* Oxford.

*Jalland, Patricia 1980: *The Liberals and Ireland: the Ulster question in British politics to 1914.* Brighton.

Jenkins, T. A. 1988: *Gladstone, Whiggery and the Liberal Party, 1874–1886.* Oxford.

Johnson, D. S. 1981: The Belfast Boycott, 1920–1922. In J. M. Goldstrom and L. A. Clarkson (eds.), *Irish Population, Economy and Society: essays in honour of the late K. H. Connell*, pp. 287–307. Oxford.

Jones, Thomas: *see* Middlemass, Keith (ed.).

Jones, William T. 1792: *A Letter to the Societies of United Irishmen of the town of Belfast upon the subject of certain apprehensions . . .* Dublin.

Kee, Robert 1972: *The Green Flag: a history of Irish nationalism.* London.

Kennedy, Dennis 1988: *The Widening Gulf: northern attitudes to the independent Irish state, 1919–1949.* Belfast.

Kennedy, Liam and Ollerenshaw, P. (eds) 1985: *An Economic History of Ulster 1820–1940.* Manchester.

Kerr, Donal 1982: *Peel, Priests and Politics: Sir Robert Peel's administration and the Roman Catholic Church in Ireland, 1841–1846.* Oxford.

*Laffan, Michael 1983: *The Partition of Ireland, 1911–1925.* Dundalk.

Larkin, Emmett 1975: *The Roman Catholic Church and the Creation of the Modern Irish State, 1878–1886.* Dublin.

*—— 1979: *The Roman Catholic Church and the Fall of Parnell, 1888–1891.* Liverpool.

Lalor, J. F. *see* Marlowe, N. (ed.).

Lee, Joseph 1989: *Ireland, 1912–1985.* Cambridge.

Lecky, W. E. H. 1912: *Leaders of Public Opinion in Ireland.* Vol. II.

Henry Flood, Henry Grattan. London.

Loughlin, James 1986: *Gladstone, Home Rule and the Ulster Question, 1882–1893*. Dublin.

Lyons, F. S. L. 1960: *The Fall of Parnell*. London.

____ 1968: *John Dillon: A Biography*. London.

*____ 1971: *Ireland since the Famine*. London.

____ 1977: *Charles Stewart Parnell*. London.

____ 1979: *Culture and Anarchy in Ireland, 1890–1939*. Oxford.

MacDonagh, Oliver 1988: *The Hereditary Bondsman: Daniel O'Connell, 1775–1829*. London.

*____ 1989: *The Emancipist: Daniel O'Connell, 1830–1847*. London.

McDowell, R. B. 1952: *Public Opinion and Government Policy in Ireland, 1801–1846*. London.

MacIntyre, Angus 1965: *The Liberator: Daniel O'Connell and the Irish Party, 1830–1847*. London.

Mac Suibhne, P. 1961: *Paul Cullen and his Contemporaries*. Vol. I. Naas.

*Mansergh, Nicholas 1975: *The Irish Question, 1840–1921*. London.

Marlowe, N. (ed.) 1918: *James Fintan Lalor: Collected Writings*. Dublin.

Martin, F. X. 1963: *The Irish Volunteers, 1913–1915*. Dublin.

Martin, F. X. (ed.) 1967: *Leaders and Men of the Easter Rising: Dublin, 1916*. London.

Martin, F. X. and Byrne, F. J. 1973: *The Scholar Revolutionary: Eoin MacNeill and the making of a new Ireland*. Shannon.

Matthew, H. G. C. 1990: *The Gladstone Diaries*. Vol. XI. Oxford.

Middlemass, Keith (ed.) 1971: *Thomas Jones, Whitehall Diary*. Vol. III. *Ireland*. London.

Miller, D. W. 1973: *Church, State and Nation in Ireland, 1898–1921*. Dublin.

*____ 1978: *Queen's Rebels: Ulster loyalism in historical perspective*. Dublin.

Mitchel, John n.d.: *Jail Journal*. London.

Mitchell, Arthur 1974: *Labour and Irish Politics, 1890–1930*. Dublin.

Mitchison, R. 1982: *A History of Scotland*. London.

Mokyr, Joel 1983: *Why Ireland Starved: a quantitative and analytical history of the Irish economy, 1800–1850*. London.

Moody, T. W. 1981: *Davitt and Irish Revolution*. Oxford.

Morgan, Austen 1991: *Labour and Partition: the Belfast working classes, 1905–1923*. London.

New History of Ireland 1989: Vol. V. i: *Ireland under the Union, I,*

1801–1870, ed. W. E. Vaughan. Oxford.

Nowland, K. B. 1965: *The Politics of Repeal: a study of the relations between Great Britain and Ireland, 1841–1850*. London.

—— 1969: *The Making of 1916: studies in the history of the Rising*. Dublin.

O'Brien, Conor Cruise 1964: *Parnell and his Party, 1880–1890*. Oxford.

O'Brien, J. V. 1976: *William O'Brien and the Course of Irish Politics, 1881–1918*. Berkeley.

Ó Buachalla, B. 1970: 'A Speech in Irish on Repeal', in *Studia Hibernica, Vol. 10, pp. 84–94*.

O'Day, A. (ed.) 1987: Reactions to Irish Nationalism. London

O'Ferrall, Fergus 1985: *Catholic Emancipation: Daniel O'Connell and the birth of Irish democracy, 1820–1830*. Dublin.

Ó Gráda, Cormac 1988: *Ireland before and after the Famine: explorations in economic history, 1800–1925*. Manchester.

O'Halloran, Clare 1987: Partition and the Limits of Irish Nationalism. Dublin.

O'Hegarty, P. S. 1919: *Sinn Fein: an illumination*. Dublin and London.

—— 1952: *A History of Ireland under the Union*. London.

O'Leary, John 1896: *Recollections of Fenians and Fenianism*, 1968 ed. Shannon.

Ó Tuathaigh, Gearoid 1972: Ireland before the Famine, 1798–1848. Dublin.

Patterson, Henry 1980: *Class Conflict and Sectarianism: the Protestant working class and Belfast labour movement, 1868–1920*. Belfast.

—— 1989: The Politics of Illusion: republicanism and socialism in modern Ireland. London.

Plunkett, Sir Horace 1909: *Ireland in the New Century*. London.

Porter, J. L. 1871: *The Life and Times of Henry Cooke*. London.

Reynolds, J. A. 1954: *The Catholic Emancipation Crisis in Ireland, 1833–1829*. New Haven.

Shannon, Richard 1989: Gladstone and Home Rule: 1886. In Lord Blake (ed.), *Ireland after the Union*. London, pp. 45–59.

Solow, B. L. 1971: *The Land Question and the Irish Economy, 1870–1903*. Cambridge, Mass.

Steele, E. D. 1974: *Irish Land and British Politics: tenant right and nationality, 1865–1870*. Cambridge.

Stewart, A. T. Q. 1967: *The Ulster Crisis*. London.

—— 1981: *Edward Carson*. Dublin.

Swift, Jonathan *see* Davis, A. (ed.).

Thackeray, William Makepeace 1842: *The Irish Sketchbook, 1842.* 1990 ed. Gloucester.

Thornley, David 1964: *Isaac Butt and Home Rule.* London.

Tone, Theobald Wolfe *see* Hobson, Bulmer (ed.).

Townshend, Charles 1983: *Political Violence in Ireland: Government and Resistance since 1848.* Oxford.

Walker, B. M. 1989: *Ulster Politics: the formative years, 1868–1886.* Belfast.

*Watson, George 1979: *Irish Identity and the Literary Revival: Synge, Yeats, Joyce, O'Casey.* London.

West, Trevor 1986: *Horace Plunkett: Co-operation and Politics: an Irish biography.* Gerrards Cross.

Whyte, J. H. 1958: *The Independent Irish Party, 1850–1859.* Oxford.

Williamson, P. (ed.) 1988. *The Modernisation of Conservative Politics: the Diaries and Letters of William Bridgeman, 1904–1935.* London.

*Winstanley, M. J. 1984: *Ireland and the Land Question, 1800–1922.* London.

Wright, Frank 1973: Protestant Ideology and Politics in Ulster, *European Journal of Sociology*, XIV, 213–80.

Zimmerman, G. D. 1966: *Irish Political Street Ballads and Rebel Songs, 1798–1900.* Geneva.

Index

All for Ireland League   77
American Revolution   4–5
Ancient Order of
   Hibernians   76–7
Anglo-Irish Treaty   102–3,
   106
Ashe, Thomas   95
Asquith, H. H.   85, 87, 92
Auxiliary Division   96, 99

Balfour, A. J.   58, 64–5, 75,
   81
Belfast   8, 33, 55, 61, 72,
   98–9
Beresford, Lord George   13
Biggar, Joseph   46
Black and Tans   96, 99
Blythe, Ernest   98–9
Boer War   72
Boundary Commission   103
Boyne, battle of   1
Buckingham Palace
   Conference   86
Burke, T. H.   51

Butt, Isaac   26, 34, 45–7

Campbell-Bannerman, Sir
   Henry   75
Carlton, William   63
Carnarvon, Earl   52
Carson, Sir Edward   81, 82,
   84, 88, 90, 103, 105
Castlereagh, Viscount   7
Catholic Association   12–13,
   15
Catholic Board   11–12
Catholic emancipation   7,
   10–13, 15
Cavendish, Lord
   Frederick   51
Chamberlain, Joseph   56
Charitable Bequests Act   25
Church of Ireland   1, 9, 12,
   17, 26
   disestablishment   43–4,
      56, 110
Church Temporalities
   Commission   44

Churchill, Winston 84
Civil War, Irish 106–7
Clan na Gael 88
Collins, Michael 100–2,
   104, 106–7
Congested Districts
   Board 64, 66, 76
Connolly, James 70–1, 78,
   86–8
Conservatives, British 18,
   20, 26, 28, 34, 43, 46,
   51–2, 54, 57 *see also*
   Unionist Party, British
Conservatives, Irish 15–16,
   19, 36, 39, 45, 46 *see also*
   Unionists, Irish; Unionists,
   Ulster
Cooke, Dr Henry 27
Cosgrave, W. T. 107
Craig, Captain Charles 98
Craig, Sir James 98, 100,
   102, 104–5, 110
Crawford, William
   Sharman 27
Croke, Thomas William,
   Archbishop 69
Cullen, Paul, Cardinal 42
Cumann na nGaedheal 72
Curragh incident 85
Cusack, Michael 69

Dáil Éireann 94, 106–7
Daly, James 47
Davis, Thomas 22, 24–6,
   28–9, 63, 67
Davitt, Michael 47, 64
Declaratory Act 4
Department of Agriculture

and Technical
   Instruction 66, 76
Derby, Earl of 40
de Valera, Eamon 90, 93,
   101–2, 106–7, 109–11
Devlin, Joseph 76
Devoy, John 48
Dillon, John 57, 75, 91
Downshire, Marquis of 6
Drummond, Thomas 18
Dublin 8, 55, 61
Duffy, Charles Gavan
   39–40, 69
Dunraven, Earl of 65, 75

Easter Rising 71, 87–91
Edward VII, King 68
Encumbered Estates Act 38

Famine *see* Great Famine
Federalism 27–8
Fenian Brotherhood 40–3,
   46–8 *see also* Irish
   Republican Brotherhood
Ferguson, Sir Samuel 67
Fitzwilliam, Lord 7, 9
Forster, W. E. 50
France 7, 36, 40
Franchise reform 38–9,
   51–2
French, Field-Marshal
   Lord 85

Gaelic Athletic
   Association 69–70
Gaelic League 70, 83
George III, King 10
Gladstone, Herbert 53

Gladstone, William Ewart, and the Church of Ireland 43–4; and the land question 44, 46, 50; and the Fenians 46; and Parnell 50–1; and franchise reform 51; and home rule 52–4, 56–7, 59–61
Glorious Revolution 1, 5
Gough, Sir Hubert 85
Government of Ireland Act 96–8 *see also* Home Rule Bills
Grattan, Henry 4, 11, 22, 24, 26, 27, 71
Great Famine 20, 28–35
Gregory, Lady 68
Griffith, Arthur 71–2, 91, 101–2, 107

Harris, Matthew 47
Hartington, Marquis of 51
Hicks Beach, Sir Michael 47
Home Government Association 44, 46
Home Rule Bills: 1886 52, 55, 57; 1893 61, 79; 1912 79, 82, 87 *see also* Government of Ireland Act
Home Rule Confederation of Great Britain 47
Home Rule Party *see* Irish Parliamentary Party
Hyde, Douglas 70

Independent Irish Party 40

Irish Church Temporalities Act 17
Irish Citizen Army 87
Irish Confederation 35–6
Irish Convention 90–1
Irish Councils Bill 76
Irish Free State 103–4, 106–8, 111
Irish Homestead 67
Irish Parliamentary Party 46–7, 53, 56, 61, 75–7
Irish Reform Association 75
Irish Republican Army 95–8, 103, 105–7 *see also* Irish Volunteers
Irish Republican Brotherhood 87–8, 101
Irish Transport and General Workers' Union 86–7
Irish Volunteers 83, 86–9, 92, 95 *see also* National Volunteers

Johnston, William 56

Keogh, William 40
Kickham, Charles James 41, 63
Kilmainham 'Treaty' 50–1

Labour Party, British 77
Labour Party, Irish 92
Lalor, James Fintan 38
Land Acts: 1870 44, 46; 1881 50; 1885 51–2; 1887 58; 1891 58, 65; 1903 66, 75

Land League 47–8, 51
landlords, Irish 34–5, 37,
    40–1, 45, 61, 65
Lansdowne, Marquis of 84
Larkin, James 86
Law, Andrew Bonar 82
Leader 71
League of North and
    South 39
Lecky, W. E. H. 7
Liberal Party, British 40,
    52, 54, 56–7, 59, 61, 75,
    77, 82–4, 94
Liberal Party, Irish 40,
    43–4, 55, 56
Liberal Unionists 56–8
Lloyd George, David 90–1,
    94, 99, 101–2, 104
Loudon, James J. 47

McCarthy, Justin 59
McHale, John,
    Archbishop 23, 25
MacNeill, Eoin 70, 83
Manchester Martyrs 42, 47
Martyn, Edward 68
Melbourne, Viscount 18
Midleton, Earl of 84, 90,
    104
Moran, D. P. 70–1
Morley, John 53
Morpeth, Viscount 18
Municipal corporations,
    reform of 19, 26

Nation 24, 37, 39
National League 51

National Literary
    Society 68
National schools 17–18
National Volunteers 88
Northern Ireland 103–5,
    107–8, 111 *see also*
    Government of Ireland
    Act; Unionists, Ulster

O'Brien, William 57, 73–4,
    76–7
O'Casey, Sean 87
O'Connell, Daniel 28, 34,
    62, 70, 109; and Catholic
    emancipation 10–15; and
    repeal of the Union 16,
    21–3, 26; and Whig
    reforms 17–20; and
    Queen's Colleges 25; and
    Young Ireland 29, 35, 37;
    idea of Irish nationalism
    36; death 37
O'Grady, Standish James
    67–8
O'Growney, Fr Eugene 70
O'Hegarty, P. S. 99
O'Higgins, Kevin 107
Orange Order 18–19
O'Shea, Katharine 57, 59
O'Shea, Captain William
    57, 59

Paget, Sir Arthur 85
Paine, Thomas 6
Parliament Act 78
Parliament, Irish 2, 9, 16
Parnell, Charles Stewart 62,
    68, 76–7, 92; and

parliamentary obstruction 46–7; and the 'new departure' 47–8, 50; and Land League 48–9, 64; and Gladstone 50–1, 53, 63; and federalism 52; and Liberal alliance 57–60; and the plan of campaign 57–8; and Phoenix Park murders 51, 58–9; last campaign 59–60

Pearse, Patrick 87–8

Peel, Sir Robert 20–1, 23–5, 28, 30–1, 34

Penal laws 2, 3

People's Budget 77

Phoenix Park murders 51, 58–9

Pigott, Richard 59

Pitt, William, the younger 9, 10

plan of campaign 57–8, 60

Plunkett, Sir Horace 66–7, 69, 75, 78

Poor Law, Irish 19–20

Presbyterians 1–6; and '98 rebellion 8; and repeal 27; and tenant right 39–40, 49, 55; and disestablishment 43; and home rule 55, 61

Queen's Colleges 24–5

Redmond, John 73, 75–7, 80, 82, 84, 87–92

Relief Acts, Catholic 5, 7

Roman Catholic Church 2, 3, 6, 14, 17, 40–1, 67, 73; and Fenians 41–2; and land league 48–9; and Parnell 49, 60; and Sinn Fein 72; and education 75; and Easter Rising 89; and conscription 91; and 1918 election 93; and Anglo-Irish treaty 106; position in Ulster 61, 98, 103–5, 108, 111

Royal Irish Constabulary 95

Russell, George 67–8

Russell, Lord John 34

Russell, T. W. 65, 74

Sadleir, John 40

Salisbury, Marquis of 51, 53, 58

Scotland 2, 31, 64

Seely, J. E. B. 85

Shaw, William 48

Sinn Fein 71, 76, 87, 90–5, 100–1, 106

Smith O'Brien, William 36

Smuts, Field-Marshal Jan C. 100

Solemn League and Covenant 82, 90

Spencer, Earl 53

Stephens, James 40

Swift, Jonathan 3–4, 71

Synge, J. M. 69

Thackeray, William Makepeace 30

Times, The 58–9
tithes 17
Tone, Theobald Wolfe 6,
8, 71
Trevelyan, Sir
Charles 31–2

Ulster, province 6, 26,
32–3, 39, 84
Ulster Defence Union 61
Ulster Unionist Council 74,
83
Ulster Unionist Labour
Association 105
Ulster Volunteer Force 83,
85–7, 99
Union, Act of 9
Unionist Party,
British 56–9, 64, 74, 83,
94, 110
Unionists, Irish 54–7, 74–5,
83–4, 90, 103–4, 110
Unionists, Ulster 55, 60–1,
74–6, 79, 81–4, 86, 88–91,

93, 110; and
partition 97–9, 102; and
Roman Catholic
minority 104–8
United Irish League 73, 76
United Irishmen 8, 40
United States of America 90,
97

Versailles peace conference
94–6

Whately, Richard,
Archbishop 20
Whig Party, British 17–20,
28, 31–2
William III, King 1, 2
Workers' Republic 71
Wyndham, George 65, 74–5

Yeats, William Butler 68–9
Young Ireland 22, 25–9,
36–7, 40